Forty Dollars and a Dream:
Breaking Through the Bamboo Ceiling

Niphaphone "Laura" Robertson

Forty Dollars and a Dream:
Breaking Through the Bamboo Ceiling

Published, distributed, and printed in the United States of America by Rose Gold Publishing, LLC.

ISBN: 978-1-952070-34-1

www.RoseGoldPublishingLLC.com

About the Author

"Niphaphone" - a *Blessing from Heaven*

. She has an appreciation for the beauty life brings.

. She can turn a mess into a message.

. She is an empath, a dreamer, and God speaks to her through her dreams.

. Niphaphone senses and feels everything around her, constantly analyzing what others are thinking.

- She cannot be around negativity for long before she needs to recharge.

- She is a fighter. When she is knocked down, she has the superpowers to bounce right back up and give it all she has.

- She always seeks ways she can bring value to those around her, often putting their feelings before her own, and at times she suffers in silence.

- She can be inspired to be the "life of the party" while other times she removes herself entirely.

- She craves understanding and affection. She loves deeply, suffering many disappointments and misunderstandings because of her inability to express her inner thoughts.

- She is blessed and highly favored. Whatever she can create in her mind shows up, and everything she touches turns into gold.

- She is a believer, a God-fearing woman who knows she has not won her battles on her own and that God has brought her through every trial and tribulation in her life so she can be a beacon of light and a walking testimonial!

Table of Contents

Dedication

I dedicate this book to my father, Seme "Sam", and my late mother, Chitta "Tina", who sacrificed their lives and gave up so much for me and my brothers to have a promising future. I thank them for providing unconditional, unselfish love and care for me. They did the best they could to raise me in a country that was also foreign to them. I am proud of their bravery and grateful for all they did.

To my husband, Marcello, for being there for me through good times and bad, for always believing in me and pushing me toward greatness.

To my children Asia, Tialoni, Cello, and Carmello; my granddaughter, Novi, and my grandson, Elikai.

To my brothers, Norrarak and Alisak, for putting up with me and always bailing me out of trouble while growing up. I am super proud of all their accomplishments and for being such a great role model for me to follow. To my sisters-in-law,

Bouakham and Nana, and my nieces and nephews, Arya, Amily, Kobe, Talina, and Tyrese.

Twenty-nine years ago, God knew my mother needed help with this rebellious teenage runaway that I was. So, HE sent my bonus mothers to lead me back on the right path.

I want to dedicate this book to three strong black women in my life. My momma Sonya, who took me in as a lost teenage runaway, for loving me unconditionally, and raising me as her own. Grandma Bessie, for being there and helping to make sure that I stayed on course. To momma Lorraine, who carried the torch and taught me how to love myself, grow strong in my faith, and to rely on God to get me through my most difficult days. She guided me into my womanhood, being my spiritual guidance, and always there in my good and bad times - reminding me that God is always in control.

They say it takes a village to raise a child and I am forever grateful that God gifted me with three strong mothers who helped shape me into the woman I am today.

Malcolm X once said, "*The most disrespected person in America is the black woman. The most unprotected person in America is the black woman. The most neglected person in America is the black woman.*"

No one can ever take my mother's place, but I want the world to know that if it were not for the love, strength, wisdom, and backbone of these strong, black women in my life, I don't know where I would be today.

They have shown me how to love myself.
They have shown me confidence.
They have shown me strength.
They have shown me keep God first.
They have shown me to speak up.
They have shown me to have faith.
They have shown me to have a backbone.
They have shown me to love and forgive.

To all the people from First Presbyterian Church of Kingsport, Tennessee, that overcame their hesitation and allowed God to guide their steps to rescue us from the extremely poor living conditions of the refugee camp. I am forever grateful for all the love and kindness that they poured into our family.

To all my friends and family that have supported me throughout this journey, thank you for all your continued love and support.

To my Lao community who share the same journey, I hope you will find the inspiration within yourselves to tell your stories. The world needs to learn more about who we are and bridge the gap of this racial division.

Finally, a big thank you to my dear friend and publisher, Dolly Cortes, of Rose Gold Publishing, LLC, for your guidance, your friendship, and your love. Thank you for all you have done to help me bring my story to life!

Acknowledgments

I acknowledge Jane Scott and the entire Scott family for the unconditional love they gave to our family.

A huge thank you to Jane Scott for keeping all the materials I could use in this book for the past thirty-five years.

Thank you to the *Kingsport Times-News* and Ms. Ingraham for doing such a fantastic job covering our family's story, allowing me to share those precious moments in this book.

May you rest in heaven, mom and Mr. Bodie Scott, Ms. Ingraham, and everyone who passed on that had a hand in helping us live the American dream.

I am forever grateful; you are gone but never forgotten.

My Story

In 2011 I lived in Grand Rapids, MI, where my husband was finishing up his marketing degree. In one of his elective classes, he had to choose a topic to write about. He decided to write about someone who came from another country, and the person he chose was me. That was when I questioned, "Where DID I come from? How did I get here?"

I reached for the phone.

I called my father and asked, "how did we get here and why did we come to America?" There was silence followed by a long pause on the other end of the line. He said, "I'm not sure how to answer that question. Here is a number for your sponsor, Jane. She might have some information for you." I had heard about Jane and her husband throughout our childhood growing up, but I never knew the role they played in our lives.

With an awkward feeling, not knowing what response I would get on the other end of the line, I picked up the phone and began to dial.

Me: Hello Jane? This is Niphaphone. Do you remember me?

Jane: Niphaphone? YES! It's been thirty-plus years, what a pleasant surprise! We missed you so much after you left here, but we understood why you had to leave.

Me: The reason for my call is my father gave me your phone number. My husband is working on a paper about someone from a different country for his college course, and he decided to write about me. I called my dad to learn more about our history, and he gave me your phone number. He said that maybe you have some information to share with me?

Jane: Yes, we were a part of the refugee committee that was formed by the church to sponsor a family from Laos. When you arrived, your family lived with us for a short time when your heat went out. Then, your parents heard of family in Illinois and decided it would be best to be closer to them. We were very sad, but we understood why you had to go. I think I still have a lot of stuff saved in our attic. Let me have your address, and I will do a little digging and send you what I have. How does that sound?

Me: *That would be great, thank you!*

***

On April 12, 2011, I pulled Jane's letter out of the envelope she sent, plus everything that would explain so many unanswered questions about my life. I knew that we had come to America because my parents were seeking a better life for us, but I never knew that it was so much deeper than that.

Letter from Jane:

Dear Laura,

What a wonderful surprise to receive your phone call Sunday night! You sound great, and we were so glad to get updates on all your family – we still think of each of you often and would love to see you again.

I have had a good time going through my collection of articles, pictures, letters, etc. Hopefully, what I am sending will be of interest to all of you. I think as we get older, family history means more to us than when we are young. Your family will always be very special to us.

PS. I'm still looking for pictures from you!

We send our love and prayers,

Jane and Bodie

As I pulled out the articles, pictures, and letters out of the package, one by one, my heart was overwhelmed as the tears flowed down my face. I was in disbelief that I was reading about myself. It felt like I was reading a news story about someone else. The more I read, the more it became a reality that this WAS my story! I began to sob uncontrollably.

It was so touching to learn how the love of selfless strangers changed our lives forever. They were so unselfish to take time out of their lives to sacrifice for our family, and I am forever grateful for what they did.

This discovery helped me unravel the part of my history that I never fully understood. I finally learned the truth. Our family, like thousands of other Laotian families, fled the Communist rule in Laos because it was unbearable to live under those life-threatening circumstances.

Many, like us, escaped and lived in the refugee camps of Thailand until we were sent for by an individual or an organization, which was responsible for sponsoring us in our new country and provided us with temporary assistance to help us get on our feet.

Included in the package was:

1. Jane's letter
2. Our refugee **"Bio Sheet"**
3. Correspondence from Church World Service
4. *Kingsport Times* article: **"Laotian Family Hopes for New Start in United States**: *Seme Sanavongsay and his family fled Communist rule in Laos*"
5. *Kingsport Times* article: **"The Boat People Come to Kingsport"**
6. The Summer News-Bulletin: First Presbyterian Church
7. *Kingsport Times* article: "Church Assisting Laotian Family"
8. Letter from my dad

9. Article by Judy Ingraham, church member, on our arrival to the United States
10. Pictures from when we first arrived

As you can image, that call to Jane changed my world forever. It unlocked the mystery of my entire life and upbringing. It gave me a renewed sense of where I came from and a deeper appreciation for everything our Lao community endured.

That call was the piece of the puzzle that unlocked many of the mysteries of my life. It was the answer to why I did not have a birth certificate; it was the explanation to my father's scars on his wrist from the prison ropes; and why he had metal injected in his arms to repel bullets. It also helped me understand why my parents were so overprotective and why I was sheltered from doing most of the things that my *American* friends could do.

It helped me understand why my mother was the way she was. I always sensed a loneliness inside her that I could not explain. Who can blame her? She was only twenty-five years old, a mother of three small children, when she made that life-altering decision to leave her family behind and come to America, knowing there was a chance she would never see her father, mother, and siblings ever again.

Chapter One

We Were Sponsored

We were sponsored by the First Presbyterian Church of Kingsport, TN.

Jane and her husband Bodie Scott were church members and a part of the refugee committee. The committee was formed after the church learned of the treacherous conditions of refugee camps. They were responsible for selecting a family to sponsor and helping them upon arrival.

Jane shared with me the lengthy process it took to select a family they would send for. The four ladies who were part of the committee sat over a cup of coffee in Jane's living room, combing through all the bios. She said it took them all night before they finally concluded that we would be the chosen ones.

According to what I read, we were chosen for a few reasons. One, my father was a teacher and was able to speak a little French. They would be able to secure a

French translator to communicate with my father. The other reason was because my brothers and I were so young, they thought we would adapt better to the changes of our new life in America.

***

Correspondence from Church World Service to First Presbyterian Church during our sponsorship process:

October 20, 1978

Dear Judy:

It was SO good to talk to you this morning. It is good news that you and First Presbyterian Church in Kingsport are seriously considering a refugee family. I want to help and encourage you however you need help and encouragement.

Enclosed is a packet of materials about refugee resettlement. You will see something about the desperate situation of the refugees, particularly in Indochina. You will see some examples of experiences of three of our PCUS churches, to go along with your own experience earlier. You will see information about the responsibilities of sponsorship. Finally, you will see several sheets listing the refugees for whom we are seeking sponsors right now.

I hope these lists will answer your questions about English and about job skills. If there are any particular families about which you would like to have more information, I will be glad to send those data forms.

*Do let me know how your meeting goes. I'll be thinking about you. **May God bless all our efforts to help these hurting people**. We'll keep in touch.*

Sincerely yours,

Margaret R.
Staff Assistant for World Services

***

2nd Correspondence:

January 4, 1979
Dear Judy:

Your letter arrived in the office on December 28, but I was on vacation that last week in December. So, I am just now getting back to correspondence! At the same time my secretary was out because of illness, so there was nobody to write you. Sorry about that.

I hope the panic has subsided and preparations are going along nicely for the Sanavongsay family. *I am sorry it was such a shock that the family will be arriving so soon. I did ask that they be delayed until January 15 at least, and usually that request is heeded.*

Enclosed are some sheets prepared by the Lutheran Church which will help you know more about Laotians, their heritage and background and customs.

I am having 600 copies of the bulletin insert "No Place Called Home" sent to you today.

If I get any kind of further information about your family or about their arrival date, I will let you know immediately. The logistics of getting refugees out of the camps and onto the charter flights to Los Angeles and onto their flights to specific places in the United States must be extremely confusing. We TRY to give a week or ten days' notice, but sometimes it is more like 24 hours.

*It will all work out fine, even though with more time I am sure you would feel better about it. But the important thing is to get the **refugees out of those terrible camps** as quickly as possible-so others can be accepted.*

My thoughts and prayers are with you as you get involved. May 1979 be an exciting, growing year for you all as you risk a bit and give yourselves away!

Sincerely yours,
Margaret R.
Staff Assistant for World Service

Our Refugee Bio Sheet:

The bio sheet detailed our registration to the refugee camp. The date of our arrival to the Ubon camp in Thailand was listed as July 12, 1977. There was a long waiting list to get into the camps. During that time, I was born—homeless and outside of the refugee camp. I was just two months old at the time we were allowed into the camp.

Once in the refugee camp, it is a waiting game to leave. You must first go through a formal interview process, then your information gets sent out to all the allied countries around the world. The camps were overcrowded with people who were also waiting for their chance at a new beginning. We waited for over a year before it was our turn to be interviewed on September 18, 1978.

The bio sheet lists the names and information on the family. Seme Sanavongsay (dad) 30, Chitta Sanavongsay (mom) 25, Alisak (brother) 6½, Norrarak (brother) 3½, and Niphaphone (me) 1 yr. 3 mo. Other information listed on our bio sheet included the condition of our teeth, birthdates, education, work history, and skills.

My father's bio was listed under US Employment / Training Potential. The notes read "*needs ESL—willing to do any kind of work, interested in continuing teaching*" and for my mother, "*needs ESL, would prefer to stay home and care for kids.*"

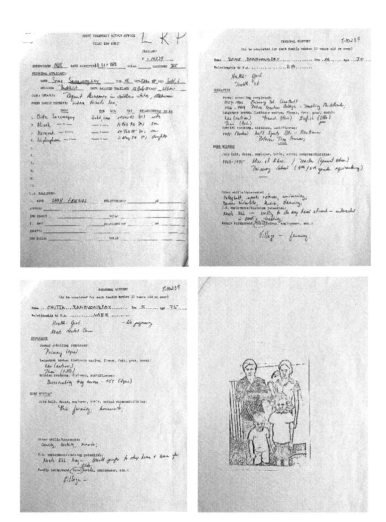

The bio sheets of families in the camps were disbursed throughout the allied countries across the world. My parents also requested to go to a southern state such as Alabama, where they learned that friends were sponsored. Our fate was in the hands of strangers who would send for us.

It touched my heart to see the correspondence between Church World Service and First Presbyterian Church. Through their hard work and collaboration, we were blessed with a new chance at life.

Judy Ingraham wrote an article in February 1979 detailing the arrival to our new home in America. I had a hard time holding back my tears when I read it for the very first time. It was a very touching article that described our sponsorship and arrival to America. Judy and Jane Scott co-chaired the committee that handled the details of the sponsorship.

Article by Judy Ingraham
First Presbyterian Church, Kingsport, TN

Considering the request to sponsor IndoChinese refugees from Church World Service, the Service Committee of our church discussed its individual concerns of financial responsibility, job placement, time involvement, language barrier, climate, and culture shock for the refugees, etc. Admittedly, we were reluctant because of the many problems that would face us, yet, in our study of the news reports we began to realize how critical the overcrowding in the refugee camps was becoming and we were increasingly moved by their desperate plight. Here we had the opportunity to provide people with a chance for life and certainly THAT had to be worth the effort. We made the decision to sponsor because of the desperate need as well as our faith in our collective talents, that, with God's help, together we surely could face any problem.

Upon receiving approval from the Session to allocate $4,000 in the budget for this endeavor, we formed a separate committee and made the selection of a 5-member Laotian family – Seme Sanavongsay (30), wife Chitta (25), sons Alisak (7) and Norarak (4), and daughter Niphaphone (1 ½). Mr. Sanavongsay had been an elementary school teacher and with his knowledge of several languages (Lao, Thai, French, and a little English) we felt their adjustment might be easier than some. We decided on this family with its young children purposefully, feeling our congregation would be most receptive to the scope of contact opportunities a varied age span would offer.

Our refugee committee divided its responsibilities into subcommittees; job, finance and legal, food and clothing, and assimilation which included language school classes, transportation, medical and dental examinations, and social contact.

I get a lump in my throat whenever I remember January 25, 1979, the day we met our family at the airport, approximately six weeks from the date we sent for them. Our welcoming contingent was composed of a small group from our committee, along with French and Thai interpreters. They had been traveling for four days from their refugee camp in Thailand – first to Hong Kong, then Tokyo, Seattle, and snowbound overnight at O'Hare Airport in Chicago. Coming direct as they did, they were exhausted and very, very cold, wearing sandals and only sweaters as outerwear to cut the January chill. We were so glad we had brought warm coats and jackets.

The Sanavongsays stayed with a family in the church for 2 days while their housing was being made ready. We searched 5 weeks to locate suitable accommodations that would be accessible to church members as well as be within walking distance to schools and shopping for them. With donations of furniture and household goods, we completely furnished and equipped their rental home. All federal housing had long waiting lists and there were few apartments available that would accept 3 children, so our housing committee had more difficulty than originally anticipated.

The Thai woman aided in stocking the kitchen larder and donations of household goods and furniture, linens, dishes, TV, clothing, etc., have eased the financial responsibilities and we have spent very little of the budgeted money thus far.

Mr. Sanavongsay has had vocational testing and evaluation at a local social service agency. He has proved to be most skillful, as well as conscientious and is doing temporary factory work while a permanent more skilled job opportunity is being explored. He is a quick learning and we have been able to communicate with humor, at both of our faltering, in simple sentences, written and spoken.

The family has already assumed paying for their food, sundries, and cleaning. We have been most impressed with their resilience and independence and rejoiced with them when they were able to accomplish grocery shopping by themselves.

The Sanavongsays are charming, trusting, bright, and eager to learn and the children are enchanting. Their ability to cope with the overwhelming culture differences, language barrier, and resettlement adjustments are an inspiration. So much so, that a person in our congregation has volunteered to underwrite the expenses of a second family and we are waiting momentarily for their arrival.

I don't know who has been learning and feeling more – we or they! In these few months we have ALL grown with this opportunity to give of ourselves. In working together, we have learned the true meaning of sharing and caring and in attempting to help we have received far more than we have possibly given.

We have become friends and that is the joy! We have given birthday parties for the children and delighted in their first experience with ice cream. We have shared concern in the hospital emergency room when the little girl received an accidental concussion when playing, and the husband suffered through the unexpected oral surgery due to an impacted wisdom tooth. We have lived with them when their furnace gave out and had to be replaced (a period of 2 weeks). We have laughed together at little boys' basketball games, shared meals at church suppers, been encouraging and pleased with job interviews. They are building a new life and we of the First Presbyterian Church of Kingsport are so privileged to have a part in it!

I remember my father sharing with me that when we first arrived, we had many people in and out of the home that we were staying in. The church families, neighbors, and journalists came by to see us and show their support for our family. Many were simply curious about what we looked like, what we ate, and how we would adapt to our new surroundings.

This next article, *"Laotian Family Hopes for New Start in United States,"* mentions a short description of my father's escape from the Communist rule in Laos. I learned there were some details lost in translation. As you read further on in my book, you will learn the true story of his escape and it may bring you to tears!

Kingsport Times article: Tuesday, January 30, 1979 "Laotian Family Hopes for New Start in United States: *Seme Sanavongsay and his family fled Communist Rule in Laos*" By Gene McClelland

Unable to speak English, shivering at the unaccustomed cold, and bewildered at all the strange surroundings, a Laotian family arrived here last Thursday at noon.

At the Tri-City Airport, after a night in the waiting room of Chicago's snowed-in O'Hare Airport, they were met by a delegation of friendly folks from the First Presbyterian Church who plan to help them build a new life in Kingsport.

It's not going to be easy; members of the church group are ready to admit.

Seme Sanavongsay, the father of the three children under seven, was a teacher in Laos. He speaks Laotian, Thai, French, and a few words of English. His wife, Chitta, speaks Laotian and Thai – no English. The children understand Laotian best, although they have lived in Thailand for the past couple of years in a refugee camp.

So, when the church group met the family at the airport, they brought along members who spoke French and Thai.

The family was taken to the home of church members to rest and relax while their Kingsport home, courtesy of the church, was being made ready for them.

It was in the quiet seclusion of the Gary McGraw home on Lonewood Circle that the Times-News met the family the following day.

Communication with the mother was impossible, since there was no one there who spoke Thai, and Sanavongsay couldn't be persuaded to talk to her in the presence of strangers.

But he told a heart-rending story of escape from Communist rule by rowboat across the Meking River in the dead of night.

Speaking through French interpreter Germaine Bus, he said he had earlier crossed the river to visit friends not knowing it was forbidden at the time.

When he returned, he was accused of being a spy, and removed from his teaching position.

I believed in the old way of government, and I guess the Communists knew it," he admitted.

He said he was imprisoned by the Communists for some time, and not allowed to visit with his family. Finally, he was let out of prison and given another job. It wasn't clear what the new job was, but he was still separated from his family.

After a period of working, he was allowed to visit his family "for a vacation."

It was while he was on the vacation that Sanavongsay took his wife and the two children they then had and went to the river where he rowed the small boat about 1.2 miles to safety.

They left behind both sets of parents and six brothers and sisters. He doesn't expect to ever see them again and doesn't know whether they are living or dead.

While living in a refugee camp in Thailand, they made no attempt to write family, because of fear of Communist reprisals. Sanavongsay says there may have been some, anyway.

"I couldn't stand living under Communist rule," he says. He says they were able to cross the river into

Thailand because in 1975 the borders were not as closely guarded as they are today.

When he learned he might come to America, he says he was very happy. "I'm so happy to be here" he says through the interpreter. "Americans live well, and in Laos everyone is so very poor."

Looking around the home in which he was staying, there was wonder in the small man's eyes. "It is even more than I expected."

And although the McGraw home was winter warm, the family members huddled in warm clothing, unused to the chill of East Tennessee in January.

None could be persuaded to venture out for a sight-seeing tour of their surroundings. It was too cold out there, with snow on the ground that day.

But later, they did go out – out to a new home prepared for their arrival by members of the First Presbyterian Church. Fully furnished, the four-bedroom home includes a dining room and large living room.

"They were so pleased when they saw their new home," says the Rev. William P. Woods, Pastor of the church. *"I think they have probably never had so much space to call their own in their lives – particularly not in the refugee camp."*

And most likely, not in the small town of 500 people in Laos – Savannakhet – from which they escaped a few years ago.

"I am willing to do anything to work. I'm willing and ready to work here to make a new life. I wanted to come here because this is a free country. It's democratic, and it has liberty," Sanavongsay told a visitor his first day in this town.

Chapter Two

The Boat People

Since sponsoring our family was such a success, a second family was sponsored. In this following article, *"The Boat People Come to Kingsport,"* you will see our family along with a mother and son. The news reporters came into the home to interview the wives while their husbands were at work.

There is a very heartfelt story behind this picture. When I shared this article with my brothers, we noticed the names of the little boy and the mother in the picture. We decided to look for "Kipo" and found him on Facebook.

I shared this picture and had a very shocking response from Kipo, now an adult, and he said that picture brought him to tears. Kipo thanked me and said that his mother had leukemia and passed away three months from the release of that article. He did not have any good photos of her and carried around a watered-down photo and a distant memory. He can now put a clear face to what his mother looked like.

That touched my heart. It was a great thing that the image was in color and such a clear picture of his mother. I was so glad that we were able to find him and give him that closure.

Kingsport Times article: Friday, July 13, 1979 *"The Boat People Come to Kingsport"* By Gene McClelland

They came to Kingsport speaking little English, knowing little about the country, but not friendless. Two Laotian families who were taken under the wing of the First Presbyterian Church are becoming a part of the Kingsport community: living here, playing here, and working here.

The current mission of the church to bring foreign-born residents into acceptance by the community is not new for First Presbyterian.

A few years ago, a Vietnamese family was brought to Kingsport and lived about six months before moving to California where the opportunities where greater for suitable work for both the father and mother of the four-child family.

The church keeps in contact with the first family, and they are doing well.

And when the need arose for sponsors for Laotian families, the church was ready, willing and able to take a stand once again.

"If we take our commitment to Christ seriously, this is not the kind of problem we can ignore," said John Hay, community minister and administrator for the church. The original call for sponsorship of foreign families came from the denomination headquarters in Atlanta, said the Rev. Bill Wood, pastor of First Presbyterian.

"We had a contact person in Atlanta who had a list of people we might wish to sponsor, and we were able to choose a family whose needs we felt we might be able to fill," he said.

When the call went out for Boat People sponsors, the church felt it should respond, said Wood. The first Laotian family was chosen and brought to Kingsport, and then a member of the church-who must remain anonymous, since this was a stipulation to taking the action-agreed to bring a second family here, assuming all the financial responsibility.

And having someone nearby who speaks their own language has helped both families adjust.

Both men have found work and were working the day the Times-News stopped by to take pictures of the rest of the family.

The Sanavongsay family – Seme, (the father) 30, Chitta, (the mother) 25, and children Alisak, 7, Norrarak, 4, and Niphaphone, (the only girl in the family) 2, arrived Jan. 25 when there was snow on the ground. The colder climate here chilled them to the bone.

And perhaps the knowledge they were entering a different culture, leaving all that was familiar behind, added to the chill they felt. But they got a very warm welcome from the church family.

They stayed several days with one family, and then moved to an apartment of their own. No sooner had they moved in that the heating system broke down. They were taken into the home of Mr. and Mrs. Paul B. Scott Jr., members of the church, helping the family get settled, where they stayed for 12 days.

"This whole adventure has been so exciting," said Jane Scott. "They're so bright and such warm and friendly people, and it's fun to watch them learn. Chitta (pronounced Kit taw') would cook Laotian foods, and I would cook American foods while they were with us, and then we would share, each learning something about the other's eating habits."

"And I feel it's been a good experience for the church, especially the youth. The Middlers had a car wash to raise money for Niphaphone's hospital expenses when she had an accident and hurt her head," she said.

The Xaysongkham family arrived March 31. There is Phim, the father; Khamnang, the mother, and Kipo their 4-year-old son; and Somxay Phetsomphon, Khamnang's 13-year-old brother.

Almost as soon as the first family arrived they enrolled in English classes. The father knew a few words before he came and speaks French fluently. Alisak enrolled in kindergarten and picked up a lot of English there. He will be entering first grade in the fall.

Both families have been included in a number of church and family outings. They love picnics, and the women are learning to cook American food, although both like going to local import store to get foods they're more familiar with.

While they are getting established and learning about the community, members of the committee help them shop, take them to the doctor and the dentist, and gently guide them in learning about life in Kingsport.

Both families seem happy, and the children have all fallen in love with the American children's books that are readily available in both households.

"We just feel like they're a part of our family," said Jane Scott. "There's a corps of people involved on a day-to-day basis with helping them. They love to play games, canoe, and fish. I'm not sure having them here isn't doing us better than it is them. It's been so much fun."

Hay feels the involvement with the Laotian families is "very necessary and tangible way to demonstrate Christian concern for others" even though it affects only a couple of families. "There are other ways to demonstrate concern for others, of course," he said.

"But the whole Bible gives emphasis on Christ's concern for the poor and needy, and this is one of the ways to show that concern today, I only wish more people and more churches would get involved.

"What we are doing here is almost literally providing life for these people. The federal government is allowing as many as 14,000 a month to come into this country, but each who comes must have a sponsor. We

have the resources and the affluence to do it, and I think it's a mission we should be doing," he said.

And Wood said he's constantly amazed at the stamina of the families who were selected and brought to Kingsport by First Presbyterian. "They arrived here not knowing the language, moving into a culture completely foreign to them, and they are adjusting.

"For me, personally, it's a very significant thing in the life of our church to be associated with these families. It relates us to the problems of the world, and the people in our church can see the significance of world problems by working with these people. It's a mission we can be involved with which gives us a sense of accomplishment as we see them grow and develop."

Article: CHURCH ASSISTING LAOTIAN FAMILY

Boat people.

They arrived in Kinsport Thursday, unable to speak English, knowing no one here, but willing to try to make a new life here among all the "foreigners."

And the concern of the First Presbyterian Church congregation is giving this Laotion family, which has been living in Thailand since 1977, that opportunity.

The Sanavongsay family, a father and mother and three young children, will be staying with members of the church until a house has been cleaned and furnished for them. Church members are donating the furnishings, and are in need of chests of drawers, end tables and lamps, said Mrs. John Ingraham, one of the committees on housing the Laotians.

The father, Seme Sanavongsay, was a teacher in Laos and knows a little English, Lao, French and Thai languages. Church members have pledged to try to find work for him, although he already knows he won't be able to teach because of the limited knowledge of English.

"The church is underwriting the whole thing," said Mrs. Ingraham. "Their moving here...finding...him a job...helping them establish a new life."

After learning we had family in Illinois, we decided to move. We had a couple of family members drive a U-Haul to Tennessee to pick us up. My father recalls the experience. Our entire family of five were riding in the front of the U-Haul, traveling over eight hours to our new destination. He said it was not a very fun trip.

Article: In the Summer News-Bulletin: First Presbyterian Church

On July 26, Seme & Chitta Sanavongsay and their 3 children left Kingsport to begin a new life in Elgin, Illinois – outside Chicago. They will be living close to the families of one of Seme's brothers, several cousins, as well as a former Laotian village friend who has been in Chicago for 3 ½ years. The friend drove from Chicago to get Seme's family. Seme will be working at Hager Pottery in Elgin.

Seme expressed his gratitude and appreciation to this church for helping his family begin their new life in America. Although we will miss the Sanavongsays, we are thankful that we could share in their lives these past six months and are pleased that they are going to be reunited with family and friends in which appears to be a very good situation for them.

Over the years, my father kept in touch with Jane and Bodie Scott. Bodie was the president of his company,

Oxygen Service Company. He came to visit us whenever he would make a trip to one of his offices in the Chicago area. I saw him over the years, but I still didn't understand the role that he played in our lives.

In the package, I found a letter that my father sent to Bodie after we arrived in Illinois:

Dear sir,

I am sorry about I'm moving too fast, and I didn't see you before I moved. I think of you, Jane, Elizabeth, and Bowen very much. You have a good helping to me and my family. Niphaphone talk about Elizabeth every day. Now I learn in YMCA school about English.

Next month I will learn a skill because I need skill. I think in USA if we don't have a skill very hard to find a good job. I will learn welding in YMCA next month. Now I have a test in Leeward $4.10/hr but not yet.

In Elgin is bad city because have a lot of stranger, different color people. Don't have too much church. I like Kingsport because very much church and very much good people. If I have a skill I will be back to Kingsport.

Thank you, sir,

Seme Sanavongsay

Chapter Three

Our Reunion

In September 2014, a few years after we reconnected, we learned Bodie Scott had passed away. My brothers and I dropped everything to make sure we were present for the funeral to pay our respects. Both of my brothers flew in from California and I flew in from Michigan, where I was living at the time. When we landed, we went over to the Scott family home. It was a very touching reunion with Jane and her children, Elizabeth and Bowen. It was nearly thirty-five years since Jane and I had our last hug, but I felt the love never left our side.

I felt so much love from everyone that even after thirty years, it was like we never left. Jane showed us around the home where we lived for two weeks while our furnace was getting fixed. Jane said that she had plenty of room in her home for us, but we decided to sleep in one room. We were accustomed to all being close together and we did not want to be separated.

We met a lot of people at the Scott home during our visit. People were coming by to pay their respects. Many of the visitors were also present during our arrival to Kingsport in 1979 and remembered our story. The word got out that we would be in town. and *Kingsport Times News* reached out to ask if we would come down to the station for an interview.

The day following our interview, we walked out of our hotel room into the lobby, and when we looked at the newspaper stand, there sat our picture staring back at us. Thirty-five years later, we were back on the front page of *Kingsport Times*, this time to share where we are now.

https://archive.is/kAlOY#selection-2437.0-2455.13

Laotian family returns to region years after a local church sponsored their trip to America

September 27ʰ, 2014 2:00 pm by NICK SHEPHERD

It has been 35 years.

- *35 years since a Laotian family arrived in a new country on a cold January day, without family and unable to speak the language.*
- *35 years since two parents with three children fled a civil war that ravaged their homeland.*
- *35 years since they left a refugee camp in Thailand and made their way 8,802 miles to a small city in the mountains of East Tennessee called Kingsport.*
- *35 years since the family was sponsored by First Presbyterian Church for their trip to America and taken in by Bodie Scott and his family for a time.*
- *35 years since one family's life changed forever.*

So, when Nor Sanavongsay, Alisak Sanavongsay, and Niphaphone Sanavongsay-Robertson, the three children of Seme and Chitta, heard that Scott passed away last Saturday, they dropped everything to come to his funeral.

"He was a great man from what I remember," Nor said. "He was so nice and kind all the time."

The Sanavongsay family lived in Kingsport for most of 1979, staying from January to August before they moved to Elgin, Ill., where they would live for the next 30 years.

The family had a harrowing journey to even get to the United States. In the mid-1970s, travel across the Mekong River in Laos was forbidden. Seme crossed the river to visit friends, and when he returned, he was accused of being a spy and removed from his position as a teacher.

He was imprisoned and not allowed to visit his family. He was eventually let out of prison and given a job. He could visit his family for a vacation after he worked for a while. During that visit, Seme took his pregnant wife and two children to the Mekong River, where he rowed a small boat about 1.2 miles to Thailand, leaving behind parents, brothers, and sisters.

The family stayed in a refugee camp until they were told a church from Kingsport was sponsoring them to come to America.

The children were very young at the time. Alisak was seven, Nor was four, and Niphaphone was two. It was a hard transition because none spoke English and arrived in Kingsport in January was a bit of a shock.

"I remember it being very cold. It was freezing," Nor said with a laugh. "That's what I remember. Just seeing snow for the first time was magical. I was like: Where is this wonderland we are going to? It was nothing like the camps we were staying at."

One of Nor's fondest memories of his time in Kingsport was Bodie teaching him to play baseball. A picture of the two-playing baseball stayed in Bodie's office for 30 years.

Alisak, the oldest child, was enrolled in kindergarten at Andrew Jackson Elementary School.

One day at school, Alisak forgot his lunch money. He did not speak any English, so he could not figure out how to tell her about his predicament when he got to the cashier. Not knowing what to do, he did what a lot of children do, he cried. Another boy paid for his lunch, and when Alisak got home that day, he told his mother what happened.

"She gave me the money to pay him back the next day, but it was all pennies. It was a dollar's worth of pennies," he said. "I took it to school, but I didn't know how to tell the other kid that I wanted to pay him for yesterday. I had the extra money in my pocket, but I didn't know how to pay him back and tell him."

After the family moved, life happened. Alisak went to Vanderbilt for a couple of years. He then felt he needed to connect with other refugees like himself. He found other Lao people and started networking. Little by little, the group started growing, and he started an organization called LaoNet. Then he started a Lao literary group and published six books. Currently, he works for the University of California on their newest campus as a digital asset programmer. He has two children.

Nor went to Northern Illinois University to study to be an illustrator. He said he wanted to draw for comic books, but while he was in school, the Internet became popular. He switched his major to web design and graduated in 1998. He went on to work for a few companies, then in 2010, he moved to San Francisco and is currently working at Barnes and Noble. He has two children.

He also wrote and illustrated a children's book based on a Lao fable published through a Kickstarter campaign. The book publishing spurred Nor to start a nonprofit organization called Sahtu Press, which aims to print Lao stories.

Niphaphone received her bachelor's degree from Cornerstone University. She worked in for-profit education for a while, then moved into real estate management. But her mother would have some health problems, and Niphaphone would leave that position to become her full-time caretaker. She currently works as a cosmetic surgery consultant. The job gives her the flexibility to take care of her mother. She has three children and now lives in Michigan.

Seme is getting close to retiring from being a welder. He still lives in Elgin.

During their high school years, Nor and Alisak would become interested in their history and how they got to this country. Then a few years ago, Niphaphone's husband had to do a class project telling the history of his wife. That was when she reconnected with the Scott family. Jane Scott told Niphaphone she had a package she was going to send her, which consisted of various newspaper articles and papers describing the process and its journey to get the family here.

"I read through all this, and I just bawled my eyes out because of the things that are in this material I never knew about," she said. "It just really, really touches me that the church did this for our family and us."

The Scott family never lost touch with the Sanavongsay family. Every Christmas, the Scotts would send them updates and pictures, telling them about what was happening. To repay the kindness of the Scotts and the strangers who brought them here, they try and pay everything forward and be kind to everyone—and understanding what their parents risked drives the siblings to work harder.

So, when Bodie passed away, they knew they had to pay their respects. The trio says they are forever indebted to him, the church, and the city of Kingsport for bringing them to America.

"The whole town took care of us," Niphaphone said. "We're so grateful for the whole Kingsport community. Based on what I read, everybody came to help us. We're very humbled and very blessed to have had that opportunity."

The picture where Bodie is teaching my brother Norrarak how to play baseball is very sentimental. It sat in Bodie's office for the last 35 years up to the day that he was called home. That must have been an extraordinary moment for him, and he will always be very special to our family.

Chapter Four

My Father's Story

I shared with my father that I wanted to write a book about our journey to America. I knew that it was a very emotional and touching subject for him and would resurface old memories he had buried away. That was the reason he directed me to Jane when I asked for his help with my husband's school project. I explained to him that he was not getting any younger and that I needed him to share his story.

He finally agreed to open the old wounds of the past and allowed me to interview him. After hearing my father's story, it gave me a deeper appreciation for my parents. It was a long and emotional interview for both of us. He got choked up a few times, and I had to give him his moment and space before moving on to the next question.

Many people have heard of the Vietnam War. Surprisingly, most do not know about our country, Laos, or how we were tragically affected during the war. The information I am about to share is something that many of you will be hearing about for the very first time.

During the Vietnam War, there was a secret war on Laos that was led by the CIA from 1964 to 1973. The Ho Chi Minh trail running through Laos was a military supply route to send weapons and other supplies between North and South Vietnam. The US dropped more than two million tons of ordinance on Laos continuously over a nine-year time span in an attempt to stop this operation.

This earned the name "secret war on Laos" because the CIA kept it a secret from the American people. Laos was not involved in the war, but we ended up as one of the major battlefields. The bombings on our country made Laos the heaviest bombed country per capita.

The unexploded ordnance is still hurting and killing our Lao people in the present time. The bombs are being cleared away by volunteer organizations, but it will be decades before all the bombs are completely cleared.

At the end of the war, the government of Laos was very unstable. My father did not feel safe leaving my mother alone by herself while tending to his teaching position to provide for the family. She had my brother, Alisak, and was pregnant with my brother, Norrarak. My father decided to send her to stay with my grandparents in Ampur Wanyai Province, Mukdahan, Thailand. After knowing my mother was safe with her family, he went back to work in Vientiane, Laos.

On December 2, 1975, Puket Lao Communists took control of our country. The Puket Lao government ran under the leader, Kaysone Phomvihane. The Lao Communist party leader announced that they renamed the country from Royal of Laos to the Lao People's Democratic Republic. They signed agreements giving Vietnam the right to station armed forces and appoint advisers to oversee the country.

In the meantime, they took the king of Laos and his family to the north of Laos and let them die from starvation.

After returning to his teaching position, he learned that the old Royal Lao government and the Puket agreed to merge. He was sent off with Puket Lao to the north of Laos, Viengxay city, Houaphanh Province, to reeducate the new Communist regime. They called it a "Seminar" at that time.

During his prison transport, he ran into his younger brother, Leung. My uncle Leung worked as a police patrol for the old Royal Lao government and was also taken into captivity. When they spotted each other, the brothers gave each other an emotional hug, which would end up being their final goodbye. My father took the watch off his wrist and handed it to his little brother. He told his brother, "I want you to have this watch to remember me by in case I don't get out of here alive." He later found out that his brother died in the hands of the Communists.

My other uncle, Jumpa Thong, was another one who was captured. His story shook our village to the core. A Communist held a gun to his head and made him dig his own grave. The Communists were known to led by fear and intimidation. They gathered up the villagers to watch as this unfolded. When uncle Jumpa Thong finished, they let him smoke his last cigarette before they shot him from behind. He fell to his grave and they buried him alive. My grandfather, Heuang, heard that my dad, my uncle Leung, and uncle Jumpa Thong were all in captivity and two lost their lives. His heart could not take the news. He was heart-broken and the stress eventually led to a heart attack that brought him to his deathbed.

Father was held captive in a makeshift prison that was made from a bombed-out mountain (pictured below). He was severely tortured, not given enough to eat, and forced to work hard without pay. He was held hostage with a tight rope around his wrists. Those scars are still visible today.

He did what he had to do to stay alive. Many did not make it out; they were either killed by the hands of the enemies or committed suicide. My father missed his wife and children so much during his time in captivity. He knew that if he wanted to see his family again, he had to comply with their orders.

Once he gained the trust of the Communists, he was released to a less secured area where he would be allowed a little more autonomy. He worked security for that area and could go within a certain distance from the site. If you tried to escape, they would shoot and kill you.

He disliked the new regime governing Laos and began plotting his escape for freedom. At the end of June 1976, he escaped Vientiane with two of his friends, Somnuk and Mone. His friends made him a fake ID card with the name Somchanh. Together they left Vientiane, heading to Thakek City, Khamouane Province.

His friend Mone's parents lived in Taseng Ban Pong, which was near where they were heading. The plan was to ask Mone's father to help them escape to Thailand.

From Vientiane, they crossed the Nam-Meung River and walked through the jungle for two to three days. They did not want to take the main roads for fear that someone would spot and report them. They walked in the jungle until they got closer to Mone's parents' house. Mone went to the rice farm to speak to his parents and to let his mom and dad know that he was getting ready to leave. He told them about his plans to escape the country. His parents cried after learning what he told them. My father and Somnuk waited in the jungle for Mone to return. The Communist soldiers were on the hunt looking for my father. Whenever he saw them, he would hide in the trees.

While they were waiting for Mone to find his parents, they encountered three bystanders who threatened to report their escape to the Communists. My father got on his knees, begging and pleading for them to just walk away, but they continued to cause alarm and yell out for the Communist soldiers to come and arrest my father. Scared for his life, my father shot and killed the bystanders and ran as fast as he could. He felt a lot of remorse for doing what he did, but he knew that he would not have made it out alive if the Communists found him.

They were relieved once Mone finally contacted his father. With Mone's father's help, they started planning a way to cross the Mekong River and escape to Thailand. Mone's parents were afraid their son would die in front of them while making his escape. The three friends had been wandering in the jungle for five days now without provisions and survived eating wild fruits they found.

Mone and his father were still trying to plot their escape. His dad wanted to wait until everything was clear. At the time, it was the ninth month of the year and the tides were high, so it was too high for anyone to swim safely. Mone's father told them that he would leave a boat near the Mekong River for them to use to escape.

On the day of the escape, Mone's father came out to tell them that it was safe to make a run for it because the Communist army was in a meeting. At this point, they had nothing to lose. They made their decision to die if something terrible were to happen.

They finally reached the destination where Mone's father left their escape boat. When they pushed the boat offshore my father lifted the blanket and saw all the food left by Mone's father. He got down on his knees and burst into tears. He had been walking on foot for days without food and was feeling weak from starvation. Mone's father was worried about them starving and left the fruits without them knowing. Seeing the food made him emotional and it was finally becoming a reality that they were only one Mekong River away from reaching their freedom.

Mone's father knew that they had gone days without food. He left them mak-lam-ya (Lao fruits) and escape money. I can tell this was a defining moment for my father. As he shared this part, he choked up in tears. He was reliving the moment that was the turning point of his life. He turned to me and said "It is hard for me to talk about this part; my tears keep coming down. ahh, I will skip over some of this; it is too emotional." We paused. I allowed him to have his moment. Then, he continued to tell the story after a long moment of silence and holding back tears.

Mone's parent stayed behind. Like many of the elders, they did not want to leave their homeland. The civilians were not in as much danger as the soldiers or government workers of the Royal Lao government. The Communists saw my father as a threat. Anyone who worked for the old government was an enemy to them, and my father was one of them.

When they got the boat to the middle of the Mekong River, it was dark. They decided not to cross the river in the dark because they were afraid the Thailand border police would mistake them for Communists and shoot them.

They decided to sleep in a nearby island called Kaseth Island. This island had a lot of seaweed, and it was a swamp. It was hard to walk into and had a lot of trees. There was not enough room to move around. There was a lot of wildlife, and you could hear the mice and animals' chatters. They slept there overnight, wrapping their arms around each other. That night, they made a pact that if anything happened, they were ready to die together. If one person was captured, they would fight and die together.

They left the island the next morning, crossing over to Thailand to Ban Laonath. The way the current flowed they ended up in Ban-lao-na in Thailand. When they got to Thailand, they saw the border patrols. They stopped the boat near the border and raised their hands to surrender. They wanted to get arrested so they could be brought into Thailand immigration. This would get them closer to the police in Nakon-panong, where my mom's family lived. Once they reached the border, they were pleading with the Thai border patrols at the village to arrest them. The Thai patrol refused to arrest them because they were not immigration police and did not have a car to transport them to the big city. They also said the Thai government ordered them to send anyone crossing over from Laos to return.

My father and his friends lay down in the boat and told the Thai patrol to shoot them if they would get sent back to Laos. They prayed and pleaded, "Please don't send us back to get killed. If you are going to send us back, just shoot us right now," but they did not get shot. The Thai patrol saw how frail and desperate my father and his friends were and he had sympathy for them. He waved to them to come in and fed them rice and fish while he helped them make plans.

The patrolman said, "Let's do this. Right now, I do not have a car to get you to Nakhonphanom Province. Let's have you in the boat, I will cover you up and let the boat flow with the current. When you hear the immigration police officers call out for you, that is when you come out of the boat. They are the ones who will help you get into the big city. Do not stop for civilians, they may rob you."

They were exhausted so they lay low and slept in the boat while it flowed down the river. Finally, they heard three or four immigration police officers calling out to them. Mone's dad had already told them to ditch the boat once they got to their destination. He did not want it to get back to the Communists that it was his boat that aided in their escape. So, they gave the boat to the Thai patrols in exchange for help to get to Nakhonphanom Province, near where my mother was staying.

Then they got on the motorcycle with a driver that would take them to the city. It was four people: the driver, my father, and his two friends on one motorcycle. He took them to the city bus and instructed the driver to get them to Nakhonphanom Province and bring them near the taxis, not by the crowded market.

They had 400 Badt (Thai currency) that Mone's dad left for them to escape with. The taxi driver was excited to make money. My father made a stop to a relative's home on his way to reunite with my mother. The reason that he stopped there first was to ask about my mom. He wanted to make sure that she had not fallen in love with someone else and did not want to intrude if she went on with her life. He had been gone for almost two years; my mother didn't know if my he was dead or alive.

The cousin my father visited was an influential person in Thailand. He had a lot of power, like a mafioso. He didn't want my father to be arrested, so he helped with getting the necessary paperwork completed.

After they ate, they took a taxi to Ampur Wanyai to reunite with my mother and brothers. My father had an emotional breakdown. His heart was filled with joy to see that his children and wife were still alive.

Shortly after their reunion, I was born. I was their love child. I was named Niphaphone (nip-pa-pon) by my grandfather. When I was born, we were homeless and displaced. My father was not a citizen of Thailand. Therefore, I was not born with a birth certificate.

Meanwhile, the Americans were searching the area to round up all the Laotian people who escaped over to

Thailand. They set up three camps across Thailand for all the refugees who escaped post the Vietnam War.

In 1976, my family stayed with my mom's relatives until they were able to get into the refugee camp. With my dad not being a citizen of Thailand, he could not stay there for long. He did not have the proper paperwork to find work and take care of his family. He could only make money under the table, so he did not know what to do. In the meantime, he drove people around in a three-wheeler to make a little money to feed the family.

If he stayed in Thailand, my father could not make a decent living, and the kids could not attend school. We finally got into the refugee camp in 1977, after almost a year on the waitlist. I was only two months old. We were homeless and displaced, living in the refugee camp until 1979. To get out of the camp, a family or organization would have to sponsor us. We applied for sponsorship to a lot of places, wherever they would take us. We all stayed in the camps until we could get accepted.

In the refugee camp, we had two fish to share for every six people. The United Nations fed us, but we also had some help from my uncle, Noudeng. My uncle helped with disbursing the food and when some of the freedom fighters left to go back to Laos, my uncle put some of their food aside to feed our family.

The freedom fighters would be gone for fifteen days at a time. They would go in the jungle in Laos at nighttime to bomb the Communist base and take their weapons. That was when we ate better than most days. We were desperate to fight and get our country back. It was a difficult battle as the Communist army were too strong to take down.

My father said that the hardest thing to do was to leave his homeland. As he said, "There's no place like home." He said, "Just like my birds in the cage, we try to put everything in the cage to make them feel at home, but that's not where they belong. It's not like in the jungle where they can be at home and fly freely."

We got news of sponsorship opportunity that would bring us to France. We were excited to get out of the camp and celebrated our departure day. Then, my father looked over the shoulders of the administrator and saw us on another list. This one was a sponsorship to America. It was our ticket to the AMERICAN DREAM!

Father had already signed off on our discharge paperwork to go to France, so he wasn't sure if he lost his chance to go to America. Immediately, he ran after the administrator, Somsack, and said, "Brother (aye) Somsack, can I please switch to America? I already signed off to go to France." Somsack took my father to the office and yelled at him. He said, "Why did you register to so many different places, messing me up erasing and changing, first you want to go to France, now America!" My father just let him fuss because he was thrilled that Somsack was going to make that change for him.

We finally set out for our life-changing journey to America in January 1979. The day we arrived; it was in the middle of a heavy snowstorm. People were off work and there was like 25 inches of snow. The planes did not run, so we had a layover at O'Hare Airport and slept at the airport gates. We each had one set of clothing. My father escaped to save his own life, we lost the war, we had to leave everything behind, and we did not have a penny in our pocket. **When we got to America, the immigration authorities gave us $40.00 to fund our trip. We came with *Forty Dollars and a Dream!***

My father shared his memories of our days in the refugee camp:

Dad: We all stayed in the camp together with other family and friends that escaped. The camps were built like this: a very long area, everyone built their own beds with sticks; it was like a hall, hundreds of people in each area, over twenty thousand in the camp in Ubon. We all stayed there together in each of our little sections with uncle Noudeng. They came in the camps first.

After I escaped and met up with your mom we came to stay at the camp. While I was away your mom stayed with her family. She is Thai, so she stayed with her parents. Her parents did not want her to come with me to the camp. I said I had to take care of my kids. I have nothing to raise my kids here. I said I have to have an education; I can't buy anything for the kids here. Only your mom, she grew mangos to go sell to have enough for medicine when you're sick. Your grandpa raised chickens to feed you guys the eggs.

There are certain areas of Thailand that were once part of Laos. The Lao people that were separated became Thai natives and they are called "Khon Isan." My mother's family was Isan.

Nor was called "gecko" because when he was climbing and falling, he hung on. Your brother Tuy, he couldn't climb. He would just fall to the ground. Tuy wasn't as smart, he was slower. One time he was about three or four years old, he threw a rock to the honey cone and his friends did it too. His friends ran away and Tuy just stood there. The bees surrounded him and he had all those bee stings that almost killed him.

Me: *Dad, how come in the Kingsport Times newspaper, it said that you escaped with mom?*

Dad: *It was lost in translation; I was speaking to them in French at that time and that is how they interpreted it. This is what happened. If it was translated by a Thai interpreter, then it would have been translated correctly.*

Chapter Five

My Aunts

The camps were overcrowded with people and long waits to get in. Each family was given an area where they would turn into temporary homes. Their refugee bios would be sent worldwide to allied countries, and they would have to wait for a family to sponsor them. It is almost like an adoption process. The sponsoring families had to agree to help the refugees get on their feet.

While we stayed in the refugee camp, we relied on the aid of donations and volunteer workers. The camps were overcrowded and there was not enough food to go around. My mother told me that whatever moved, we would eat for dinner. My father made a living working under the table, driving a three-wheeler for a little cash. He made about twelve baht each day driving people around in the three-wheeler, and he would bring the money back to my mother and aunts. The women would take the money down to the market and buy food. Then, they would bring their purchased products to the camps to sell in hopes of making some profit.

When I started to explore my history, I asked a couple of my aunts to share what they remembered. By the way, in the Lao culture everyone is considered your family—aunt, uncle, brother, sister—some are blood relatives, and some are not. That is the type of love we share in our community.

One of my aunts shared with me her horrific experience of childbirth in the refugee camp. She said that when she was in labor, she thought she would die on the table. There were inadequate health care resources available during that time. She recalls being on the table with her arms and legs tied to a pole, and was told that if the baby did not hurry up and come, they could not help her, and the baby would die.

They had a line of people that needed help as well. Right when they were ready to give up, the baby—my little cousin—pushed her way out. However, her umbilical cord was wrapped around her neck. The health care aide had to do an emergency C-section. This was not your typical C-section. They poured alcohol on my aunt's belly and cut her stomach open with a knife to pull the baby out. They untied my aunt and told her to get off the table so they could help the next person. My aunt said she was in so much pain as she gathered her stomach and limped away. The baby was premature and came out like a little bird.

My other aunt shared her story as well. With tears rolling down her cheeks, she relived horrible memories. She shared a story of when they still lived in Laos during the Communist rule. She left to work and left her five-year-old daughter home with a babysitter. When she returned home from work, she found her home empty. She immediately felt something was wrong. She searched all over the house for the sitter and her baby girl. There was no one in sight. She went outside to search around the house. After searching for hours, she found her slain firstborn child with her throat split open.

Until this day, she still does not know what happened to the sitter, but that image of her baby still haunts her. Her baby's necklace was missing, and the babysitter was never seen again.

In the midst of trying to hold back tears, she told me that she was proud of us. She was proud to see all of us living a better life than what we left behind. When she is laid to rest, she said that she can rest with a smile on her face knowing that all her sacrifice was not in vain.

Chapter Six

My Childhood Experiences

When we learned that we had family in Illinois, we relocated to the Chicago suburbs. We lived in a small town called Elgin. We found a small studio apartment for our family of five and went on public assistance. I was to young to realize we were so poor. We lived in a cockroach-infested apartment but compared to the extreme living conditions that we escaped, we were so much better off.

My early childhood experiences in America were filled with great memories. As more and more Laotian refugees found their way to America, many made Elgin their new home. My family and I lived in a community surrounded by relatives. Of course, some were blood, and some were not—but we were still family. We survived as a tight community and helped lift each other up.

I went to a bilingual school with about twenty other Lao refugee children. Once I graduated from my bilingual kindergarten, I was introduced to public school, which was a terrifying experience for me. I had extreme separation anxiety from being away from my mother. Whenever my mother dropped me off to school, I would do everything in my little power to kick, scream, and grab onto her while being pulled away by the teachers. My teachers had to call my mother just about every day because I would not stop crying. It took a while, but I eventually got over my anxiety.

As we all got older, our parents found better jobs in the factory. We slowly started moving out of the run-down neighborhood that we lived in and began to get more accustomed to our new way of living. We were still a very tight community. We had many get-togethers for birthday parties and events. Most weekends, we had a full house. The adults would drink and gamble while the children ran around and played.

I loved every minute of my childhood. I was daddy's little girl and a tomboy. I loved to go fishing with my father and put the worms on the hooks. I would walk in the creek to catch crawfish. I would climb trees to pick crab apples. My two older brothers would often tease me, and I would cry to my parents until I got my way. I was a spoiled little girl and always cried for whatever I wanted. I was so spoiled that I earned the nickname "e-na-gnaw" which means pouty face.

My childhood experience consisted of school, home, and family functions. My father was strict, and I was not allowed to do anything else outside of school. We also did not have the disposable income to do any extras like eating out or going to the movies. The first and only movie we saw as a family was *Good Morning Vietnam*. I did not know it back then, but now I understand why that movie was so significant for my father to bring us to watch as a family. It reminded him of what he had experienced living through the Vietnam era himself.

It was tough growing up with the name "Niphaphone." I had a hard time learning how to spell my first and last name, Sanavongsay, in English. When my parents came to America, with their lack of English, they did not realize that the "PH" was an "F" sound. I was often teased for my name and many people had a hard time pronouncing it. I knew every time a new teacher was about to call my name, because there would be a long pause before they attempted to pronounce it, calling me "NIFAFONE" or "Niaphony." I got used to it. My family called me, Phone, "Pon" for short. When my parents got their US citizenship, I was able to change my name. That is when I adopted the name "Laura."

Laura became my legal middle name. I was happy to finally be able to have an American name like my friends at school.

I remember a part of my childhood that was not so favorable. **I was often bullied and harassed because of my ethnicity. The infamous chant was "Chinese, Japanese, look at these!" with the bullies pulling their eyes back to make fun of my Asian descent.**

I wore a lot of hand-me-downs to school or clothes that my mother would sew for me. I was often criticized for how I dressed and my off-brand shoes.

I had one classmate who bullied me the most. He would throw spitballs at me and often pulled my chair underneath me to watch me fall to the ground. I was so used to being teased and taunted by my brothers, I just thought it was kids being mean and had no understanding of racism.

I had an encounter with my elementary school teacher that made such an impact that after almost forty years, I still remember it like it was yesterday. Our school was overcrowded, and our classroom was in a mobile unit in the parking lot of the school. It was right after music class. When the music teacher left, we were transitioning to another subject. Every one of my classmates was talking while we waited for my teacher to come in the room.

I happen to be singing a song that was stuck in my head from music class.

The teacher turns around and yelled to the classroom "WHO'S HUMMING?"

Everyone pointed their fingers toward me.

She yelled at me and said "Laura! Go to the office!"

I questioned her, "Why?" and she did not like that.

She began to get more frustrated and stomped over to the door.

She opened the door to let me out and said, "DO I NEED TO CALL THE OFFICE TO TELL THEM YOU'RE COMING OR ARE YOU GOING TO BE ABLE TO MAKE IT THERE ON YOUR OWN?"

I replied, "No, I can walk."

As I turned to walk toward the door, she yelled at me again, and said, "TURN AROUND AND APOLOGIZE TO THE CLASSROOM!"

I turned around and said, "Sorry, class!" and continued to walk out the door.

She followed me out the door of the mobile unit and slammed the door behind us.

When we were both outside, she watched as I walked away heading toward the school building.

As I walked away, she yelled with her loudest voice, "YOU DON'T DESERVE THIS COUNTRY!" I turned around and saw her fingers pointing towards me as her entire body turned red and trembling, her face was filled with so much anger and hatred. At that moment, I knew she was angry, but I did not know that I was witnessing an act of racism.

I WAS NOT a bad kid, had never gotten in trouble at school, but at this very moment, I was so upset that I turned around and gave her the middle finger!

I continued my walk to the principal's office. Mrs. Jones was an African American principal and I was one of her favorite students. She had that personality that everyone probably felt they were her favorite!

I remember being in Mrs. Jones's office and I told her what happened. She looked angry. Not at me, but I felt there was anger toward that teacher for what she did. Mrs. Jones turned to me and said "Sweetheart, you are not in trouble. I want you to sit here with me for the rest of the day and just draw me something nice."

When I told my dad what happened, I remember him trying to explain racism to me. He said, "Honey, some

Americans like us, but there are some that do not like people with dark hair."

They did not like me because I was different...I was TOO ASIAN.

WHERE DO I BELONG?

I was in my preteen to teenage years when life started to take a considerable turn for the worst. I was very sheltered by traditional Laotian parents who had this false hope that I would be the perfect traditional child. That is where the conflict came in. Being raised in America, I did not know how to be an ideal conventional Lao daughter.

My parents would stress how important school was and that nothing else mattered. I was not allowed to go anywhere but home and our family gatherings. I remember a time when I went bowling with my cousin. My father found out, and he came to pull me out of the bowling alley in front of everyone. We were not allowed to do any extra activities, and especially not with boys. They often stressed that they did not want me to end up in a factory and working hard as they did. School was all that mattered.

When I got to high school, I started to feel resentment toward my parents. I wanted to be like my friends, and I started to rebel. I did whatever I wanted to do against my parent's wishes and became the black sheep of the family and in my community. Many of the other children were no longer allowed to play with me. This isolation pushed me further and further away from my community. I was skipping school, failing classes, and did not care.

I was ridiculed by a few people in my community for my differences. They faulted me for not maintaining my cultural standards. I started to befriend many Hispanic and Black classmates, and I also had a few

Caucasian friends. I did not know where I belonged anymore.

At first, I was too Asian for the American community, then I became too American for the Asian community.

It got worst once I reached high school when I dated *the first black guy.* I did not see him any differently. I found him to be a nice guy who I thought was funny, someone that I could relate to.

When we started dating, I found myself being followed around in the hallways of my high school. I was taunted and bullied. I was called names like "Nigger Lover" and "Slut." I was being harassed at home as well, with phone calls yelling the same verbal attacks. I was in multiple fights that I did not start. It was a very crazy time for me.

The Black community was portrayed—and still is—in the media as criminals and bad people. So, in our Lao community, because we only stayed close to our community and got our information from the media, many formed a bias against the Black community based on what they heard. We were taught to fear anyone who was Black.

I had a different experience. I was pushed away from not being good enough for my own community, and I felt the most love and care coming from the Black community. I felt that I could relate to the struggle of being judged and racially discriminated against.

I was a lost teenager. I know that I disappointed my parents, and there was a lot of tension between us. I made stupid decisions, not thinking about the consequences. I was rebelling and getting into trouble.

As a young teen girl, in Lao culture, we are not allowed to be with boys. My mother would also say many hurtful things to me, like, "I'm going to grab a knife and cut your face so no guys would look at you!" I would often hear their late-night fights and one time heard her say to my father, "If I knew she would turn out like this, I would have aborted her in my womb!" This series of incidents, the fights with my parents, the fights with random people, the dirty words that were spoken to me, took a very emotional toll on me. I ran away from home to escape my problems.

Chapter Seven

Dealing With the Challenge

I was dating my high school boyfriend at the time, and his stepfather was transferred to Kansas City for a job. I decided to run away from home and follow him. My original plan was to move in with my uncle but once I got to his house, he told me that I could not stay there because I had run away from home.

I knew I was not going to move back to Elgin because it was too chaotic to go back to that environment. I decided to ask my boyfriend's mother Sonya if I could live with her. After a long pause, she agreed to let me stay. My father did not want me to drop out of high school, so he made momma Sonya my legal guardian. I believe that moving away into an entirely new environment helped me hit the reset button.

Initially, we lived in the suburbs of Kansas City. I went to Blue Springs High School. When momma Sonya and her husband separated, we moved in with her mother, Grandma Bessie.

Here I was, a lost Asian teenager who was taken in and being raised by a Black family that adopted me into their home. All I knew up until this point was "all things Lao." I was raised a traditional Lao girl. I was even a part of a Lao band. I grew up eating Lao food. I went to the Lao temples. I went from growing up "all things Lao" to now attending an all-Black school, living in an all-Black neighborhood, having my first taste of black-eyed peas, pinto beans, and cornbread! I even took on the urban hairstyles!

But besides all of that, the most important thing was that my new family accepted me; they loved me, and that is what helped me get on the right track.

Momma Sonya stepped into my life at the most critical time, my teenage years. She made sure I was on track with school and all my basic needs. She cared for me and showed me how a young lady should act. She showed me how to have confidence and respect in myself and how to put myself first. She showed me the feminine things I needed to know as a young adult. She took her mother role seriously and loved me as her own.

My turnaround came in the last semester of my senior year. I broke up with my high school boyfriend and moved back home to my family. I knew how important it was for my parents to watch me walk across the stage at graduation. I was happy to make my parents proud. They had come from small villages in Laos, and many did not finish higher than first grade. In the Lao community, a high school diploma is almost the equivalent of a master's degree!

As complicated as my younger years were, there were still many great memories that I have. I had ten memories that I want to share because they were funny and innocent.

10 Fun Stories From my Childhood

1.The Cake

My mother shared a memory with me of when the heater broke in our apartment in Kingsport. The Scott family welcomed us into their home while it was being fixed. When it was time to get groceries, Jane and my mother would go to the grocery store together. Mom picked up a box of cake mix from the store. She had never seen a box of cake mix and thought that since there was a picture of the cake, that is what she would find inside. To her surprise, she opened the box up only to find powder spilling all over the kitchen!

Laughter. Mom didn't think that Jane knew why she was laughing, but both started to laugh with each other! When dad came home, he tried to explain to Jane why mom was laughing uncontrollably.

I miss my mother's innocence, and how barely having an elementary school education, she survived in America. What must've been going through her 25-year-old mind? She had three small children in a world that she knew nothing about. How was she feeling miles away from her father, mother, sisters, and brothers and not knowing if she would ever see them again? The guilt she must have felt for leaving them behind. Did she ever doubt her decision? My mother was so brave and strong for this. I hope that she is smiling down from heaven knowing that her dreams came true...her three children made it because of her!

Reflection: "Life is better when you are laughing!"

2. Family Picnic

My mother received a call from one of the church members telling her to get the kids ready for a "picnic." Mom prepared our picnic baskets, and we were ready to spend a day in the park. To my mother's surprise, we ended up at the doctor's offers with the doctors telling us to open our mouths wide. We were there for a health checkup! My poor mother misunderstood the church member, who said we were going to the "clinic" and not a "picnic"!

I still remember all the family picnics. We would find a park where we could go fishing and we would set up our gear. It was so much fun. Sometimes it was just our family, and other times we would travel with other families or friends. We just enjoyed ourselves and each other's company.

I loved picnics because I loved fishing with my dad. I was such a tomboy and a daddy's girl. The tomboy part went away eventually, but I think I will always be a daddy's girl. He still calls me "E-Nang Noy" which means little girl in our language. My father and I have a special bond. I was the youngest and the only girl. My father is my world, and I don't know what I would ever do without him.

Reflection: "Remember that money and material things run out, but making memories lasts a lifetime."

3. Ghost Stories

When we stayed with the Scott family while our heater was getting fixed, we all slept in one room. It wasn't because they didn't have room for all of us in their huge home, but because we were afraid to be separated. After living in the refugee camp for two years, we were used to always sleeping and being together since our small, confined space was all we had.

One night, my parents heard a loud banging noise, an unfamiliar sound that frightened them. They assumed that it was a ghost and thought that the house was haunted. It continued all night and the next night that noise came again. My parents would say to each other, "This home has a lot of ghosts here"! They were so scared of the house. They later learned that it was the noise from the washer and dryer. Where we came from, everything was hand washed.

I remember as a child, we always told ghost stories and we feared ghosts.

I had a guy friend named Phet (PIT). He and his brother had a life-sized doll at their house. They told me that this doll would get up in the middle of the night and walk around by itself, and I believed them. I never saw a doll that big, so I was already scared of it. Every time I saw this doll, I felt like it would follow me with its eyes. I finally stopped going over there until they told me that they got rid of that doll.

There was also this part of the neighborhood that everyone said used to be a cemetery. We were told that if we walked past it at night, we'd see hands coming up from the ground. We were supposed to run fast past it. I was so scared every time I walked by there, and I ran as fast as possible. If I walked home when it was dark out, sometimes I would even walk the longer side of the block to avoid it!

Our elementary school was also said to be haunted. It was built on top of a former cemetery. I remember in first grade, I had other Lao kids in my class. Our classroom was near an elevator that would go up and down by itself. Whenever we heard the elevator, we would be so scared.

One day, when we were sitting there in the classroom, the door opened by itself. All the students, including myself, were so scared. We screamed and jumped out of our seats when the teacher said, "Come on in…"

Our classroom was near the entrance door. It was probably someone leaving or coming in. The elevator was probably someone using it who could not walk up or down the stairs. It was our lack of knowledge and experience that made us scared and thinking otherwise. We were just frightened and fearful of the unknown. I was so afraid that I would not want to leave the classroom to go to the bathroom!

Reflection: "If you can overcome your fears, you can go through any doors of opportunities."

4. Where are the monkeys?

When I went back to Tennessee for Bodie's funeral, Jane shared a funny story with me. Jane said that the church decided to sponsor a second Lao family to Kingsport. My father finally had a friend whom he could speak Lao to. They sat in Jane's living room as they began speaking in our language. The Scott family had a large home surrounded by trees. Then loud laughter came between the two of them as they were pointing outside to the trees. Finally, my father asked, "Where are all of the monkeys?" Back in our homeland, animals roamed freely, and the monkeys lived in the jungles of Laos.

In 2003, I went back to visit Thailand for the first time after twenty-six years since I left the refugee camp. My trip also included visiting Laos. Going back to my roots was a culture shock for me. Like my father's confusion about where the monkeys and wild animals were, I was confused seeing all the animals roaming so freely everywhere! It is a different world than what we live in.

America was the only world that I knew and going back to Laos gave me an even more significant appreciation for what we had.

The one thing I envied is how they lived versus how we lived. The nice part was that they did not have a mortgage to worry about, but in speaking to one of my aunts, she only made equivalent to three hundred US dollars a month working as an elementary school teacher.

In Thailand, our US dollar was worth forty-two badt (Thai currency) at that time. I gave my cousin, a college student, about four hundred badt. That is equivalent to almost ten US dollars. He was so shocked and the expression on his face was priceless. He turned to me and said, "why are you giving me so much?" I was just like, "take it; it's only ten dollars!"

I was warned to be careful what you eat out there, but I thought it was acceptable to eat a mango off the tree. Of course, I had to dip it in some Lao sauce! That was a lesson I will never forget. I got so sick to my stomach that I ended up being rushed to the hospital. Thank goodness this happened to me in Thailand instead of Laos, because Thailand had much better equipped hospitals.

When I was in Thailand, it was around the same time that the SARS outbreak had just started. That was a scary time to be in the hospital!

I was in a room surrounded by three other sick people. I was afraid I might catch SARS from one of them. I asked my aunt if she could get me into another room. I didn't have any insurance, and my aunt turned to me and said in Lao, "You're going to be paying too much for a VIP room." I asked her what she meant by "too much," She replied that it would be one thousand, two hundred baht.

When I calculated that in my head, I realized it was a little less than thirty dollars. I told her I would pay that thirty dollars to get a VIP room! It was a lot of money for her, so I can understand. I stayed overnight at the hospital on an IV drip. I had a stomach bug and was dehydrated. When I was released, my entire hospital stay for two nights, VIP service was less than one hundred US dollars! I was supposed to stay longer, but after that experience, I took the next flight home.

The good that came out of this trip was seeing my mother's side of the family in Thailand. I met my grandparents for the first time since the day I left as an infant. That day they cried, begged, and pleaded with my mother not to take me away.

My grandfather asked me, in Lao, "how did you get here? Did you come by boat or plane?" I told him that

I came by plane. He told me that the day that my mother took me away, they were so heartbroken.

My grandfather was the one who named me "Niphaphone," a blessing from heaven. It was so wonderful to get a chance to see him before he passed on from a stroke.

5. The Whole Town Took Care of Us

When we first arrived in Kingsport, not speaking the language, my father said we did not know or understand what was going on. We had people coming in and out of the house laughing and staring at us. They came to watch us as if we were an exhibit and something that had never been seen before. Imagine just sitting in a chair and seeing one person after another coming in and out of the house. All you see are their lips moving and sounds coming out, but you have no idea what they are saying. They wanted to know everything about us: what we looked like, what we ate, and what was on our minds. We were one of the first refugees from Laos to arrive in Kingsport. We are also now a part of their one-hundred-year history book of the First Presbyterian Church.

Reflection: I am so grateful for the people of Kingsport, especially the members of the First Presbyterian Church that had a hand in rescuing us from the refugee camp. They were so selfless to sponsor our family. As I read through some of the articles that Jane sent me, they were very hesitant about sponsoring a family because of the hardship that came along with it. Then, they saw more and more news about the desperate conditions that we lived in and decided to move forward with sponsoring a family, and we were so blessed that it was our family. Being sponsored to America, to me, was equivalent to hitting the lottery. Life could have been so different for our family if they had backed out from this decision. We would have ended up in France!

One day I was playing with my brother in our apartment, and the door fell on me. I had to have stitches on my head, which explains the scar I have. I didn't know I had a slight concussion from that incident until I read in the newspaper about a Midland family doing a car wash to fundraise for my hospital bills. When it happened, my father did not know what was going on. The church family came to pick him up and drove him to the hospital. When he got to the hospital, they told him not to worry. This is another example of the kindness we experienced.

The day I opened the package from Jane, my perspective changed about so many things. It opened my eyes, and I am now intentional about looking every day at ways that I can bless someone. I do it because of how our lives changed because of the kindness of strangers. I don't want their decision to be made in vain. I want to keep their legacy alive, and with everything I do, I do it in honoring those who paved the way for me. I am here to pass on the baton and pay it forward!

6. Our move to Elgin, IL

My father's friend reached out to him while in Kingsport and told him that he should move to Elgin. He said that in Elgin, they received a salary that the government paid. My father thought that was a great opportunity and moved there. My uncle came to pick us up in a U-Haul. The six of us, my family and uncle, were cramped up in the truck's cab, and we rode from Kingsport to our new home. Once my father got to Elgin, he realized his friend's salaries were public aid and food stamps! We lived in a house next to a Mexican store. My other little cousins and I would go to the store and grab candy and leave. We always got chased out of the store, and the candy was taken away from us. We probably did not understand the concept of stealing, or maybe we did? But I bet their lives changed when these refugee kids moved into the neighborhood!

Reflection: My father was a man who did not say "no" to helping another family in need. As more and more refugees came to Elgin, many of them came to stay with us until they could get on their feet.

I love the bond that our family had for each other. No matter where we are in life, family is always there for us. When I say "family," this is sometimes not blood family. We had some families that we did not meet until the refugee camps or when we arrived in America. We still called them family and we had a close bond. It is not uncommon for us to call each other "sister" or "brother." It's a form of respect, and it is also the Lao culture that everyone becomes family.

When one of the Lao families in the community had their house catch on fire, my father offered our home as a shelter. This family of eight stayed with us until their apartment was livable again, joining our family of five plus two other relatives. There were a total of fourteen to sixteen of us in a two-bedroom roach-infested apartment.

I want to add that although our homes were filled with roaches, it was just the norm. It was a roof over our heads and much better living conditions than the refugee camps were. I remember my father telling me that the refugee camp was so filthy that I contracted a bad skin infection. If you look close enough, you can see three small craters left on my forehead.

Our parents had a survival system for everything! They had one van that was transportation for our community. Every Saturday, the kids would be at home while the parents got in the van, heading out to get laundry and grocery shopping done. The system they had going is what got us out of our position. Everyone treated one another like family and worked as a village to get us to the next level. We worked together to chase our American dreams.

We adapted, grew, and helped each other out through it all, in sickness and health.

7. We loved crab apples!

If we saw an apple tree, we would climb it and pick apples. We saw a tree in the neighbor's yard and climbed the fence to get to it. Once an angry older man ran out with his shoes in his hands, yelling and throwing them at us. We didn't know what he was saying, but we knew he was mad. We climbed down and ran away as fast as we could! That did not stop us; we kept coming back for more, but this time we were quieter about it.

Reflection: As I look back, I wonder what he would do if it happened in today's time. If he saw poor kids from around the block trying to get food from his apple tree, would he go back to his kitchen to bring us out a meal? Knowing what I know now about racism, things that I did not understand as a child, I wonder if he despised us because we were different. If we were of the same race, would he be that angry and throw shoes at little hungry children who were trying to eat? We were just little three- to five-year-old refugee kids who didn't know any better.

We were taught those survival skills at a young age— as my mother would say about our life in the refugee camps that "Whatever we found or whatever moved was our food." When you are put in a desperate position, you do things that may not be appropriate.

8. We felt safe.

We used to feel safe roaming the streets back then. I was only around three or four, and I was walking around the neighborhood alone most of the time with my dirty bare feet and hand-me-down clothes. I would find things to do and other children to play with.

I remember once when I was playing hopscotch on the sidewalk, I stepped on a big piece of glass that pierced into my toes, and I started bleeding profusely. A neighbor came and picked me up, wrapping something around my foot to stop the bleeding. I looked up at his face, and he looked scared as he hurried around the neighborhood, trying to find out where I lived. With the help of bystanders, he was able to bring me home safely.

We felt safe in our neighborhood. We were all poor, but we were rich with family and neighborly love. Everywhere we turned, we saw joy and happiness. We were one community.

Reflection: I was blessed to be a part of a movie project that highlighted our Lao story. It is called *The Lao Redemption.* I played a non-speaking part that was filmed in Elgin, in this same old neighborhood that I ran around as an innocent refugee child.

It brought me back to those childhood memories when it was safe to go outside. We played outside from sunrise to sunset, playing games like hopscotch, jump rope, tag, and whatever we could think of.

Now, we must watch our surroundings. We must travel in groups. We must make sure our doors are locked. We must not let the little ones outside by themselves.

Especially now, with all the Asian hate going around, we must be more careful. When I leave anywhere alone, I always call my children or husband on the phone. I am obsessed with keeping our doors locked, even at our place of business. It is so crazy to feel that at any minute you can become a target of violence. I pray that we get back to the days when we can feel safe again.

9. The Truth Was

As a child, I didn't know we were poor. The highlight of my childhood was every year around Christmas; we would walk in the snow down to the YWCA. The place was packed with other children waiting in line to see Santa Claus and get our little bag of toys. We were all so excited! I didn't know until I got older that we were waiting in line to get generous donations from all the kind strangers who wanted to see a smile on a poor child's face!

I had a few childhood friends in elementary school. The two that I spent the most time with were Rachel (Larcy) Ward and Andrea (Andy) Williams. I loved going over to their homes after school because they had a lot of toys. We played with their Barbie dolls and Cabbage Patch Kids. I didn't have any of my own since my parents couldn't afford them.

Reflection: I will never forget the time when I was managing an apartment community. One of my leasing consultants, Sarah, came into work and said that she had a triggering conversation with a little girl who lived next door. Sarah said that she was out in the yard, and the two little girls next door came out of the house. She asked them what they were getting for

Christmas, and they said, "We will be lucky if we get a candy bar. Mom doesn't have money to get us anything." When Sarah shared that with me, I knew we had to do something.

We rallied up donations around the office, and I volunteered to be the delivery person. I took all of the money that we raised and took it to the store. I packed up my cart with everything I thought little girls would love!

The day came, and it was time for me to go to deliver the presents. When I walked up and knocked, a lady came and slowly opened the door. I was so excited that I asked for the wrong name. She told me that I have the wrong house and that she was not expecting any deliveries. I said the two little girls' names again, and she said that they are her daughters, but they are not home right now. I asked if I could come in and that I had a surprise for them.

When she allowed me into her home, I immediately felt something was wrong. There was a bed in the living room, and she had a head covering wrapped around her head. I didn't want to ask, but it seemed like maybe she was battling some illness.

I told her that I was a secret Santa, and I was there to deliver presents to her daughters because I had heard her family was struggling to get gifts for the family. She immediately broke down in tears as I poured out all of the presents on her bed in the living room. She yelled for her husband, "Honey, come and look at this! You will never believe what is going on here!"

Her husband joined us in the living room as I took out more and more gifts. They both stood in disbelief, and what she said next made me break down and cry.

She told me that it has been rough for them financially and that she had just come back from Toys for Tots trying to fight for presents for her girls, but she was only able to grab one thing. The rest were all taken. I was blown away.

I knew that because of the kind strangers giving away toys, I had had the best Christmas year after year.

I was glad that I was able to be a blessing and pay it forward. When the girls got home, the mother took a picture of them and sent me their smiling faces. That was enough to make my heart melt.

Reflection: You may not realize how blessed you are—
I choose to be grateful every day for all that God has
given me. Your bad is someone else's best.

10. She reminded me of my mother

When I would walk to my childhood friend Andy's
home, I noticed an elderly Caucasian woman living
alone. She always waved to me and said "hello." One
day, she invited me to her home. I sat in her kitchen
on the table, and she served me a cup of 7 Up with her
homemade cookies. I could tell she was lonely. She
shared with me that her husband had passed away and
that she had left everything the way that he left it; even
his recliner still had his last cigarette. She said she was
alone, and her children lived far away. She didn't see
them that often, so I kept her company. We developed

an extraordinary bond as I started to visit her regularly. She always had her cookies and 7 Up ready for me, and I knew that I made her smile when I went to see her.

Reflection: She reminded me of my mother in her last days.

My mother had some underlining health complications. Then, she had a bad fall that left her confined to the bed with limited mobility. I knew that my mother, too, felt loneliness. She loved it when we came around and kept her company. I didn't want my mother to feel like my friend, alone.

At that time, both my brothers and I lived out of state. My father was still working, so she spent the day at home alone. When she had her fall, she could not go home if no one would be home with her. She needed 24-hour care. I decided to move my mother to

Michigan and dedicated myself to make sure she was well taken care of and that she felt loved and appreciated.

I brought mom to Grand Rapids, Michigan, and I remember the mistreatment we received at the hospital. My mother was having issues with swallowing, and she would refuse to eat. After days of trying to get her to eat, I took her to the emergency room. They kept sending her home and the same thing would happen. They would admit her sometimes and then send her home. I ended up having to bring her back to the hospital, and they would send her home again. Finally, I brought her back to ER after she was still not eating. This was going on for a month of barely holding food down. This time, I demanded that she be admitted and to perform a complete evaluation. They were so upset at me for even demanding that request.

They finally admitted her after eight hours of waiting. During that wait, something did not feel right. My mother started to hallucinate. I believe she was very dehydrated, even though the hospital staff said all her vitals were normal.

My mother started doing and saying things that were out of character. I was scared. This was when I realized that she was either dehydrated OR she was really at the end of her life and seeing some paranormal visions. If you are an easily frightened person, you may want to skip ahead!

She was staring into the ceiling, and she turned to me and said, "Do you see that devil in the ceiling?"

That gave me the biggest chills! I said, "No, mom, you're just seeing things."

She said, "Look, it's right there." She pointed to the ceiling.

My daughter, Asia, was in the room with us. Asia and I were getting scared at this point. Asia turned to my mom and said, "Grandma, pray to Jesus for it to go away."

My mother turned to Asia and said, "It says it doesn't believe in Jesus."

Then, I was videotaping this entire encounter when my mother turned to me and said in a strange, scary voice that did not sound like herself, and she told us, "Hee –

sue- pie - miy" (your private parts are on fire!). This was definitely not something my mother would say. Asia was so scared she flew out of that emergency room like she had seen a ghost!

I believe she was genuinely dehydrated from barely eating or drinking for nearly a month. I told the ER staff that I refuse to take her home and let her die on me.

They told me that they were only admitting her for observation, that there was not much they could do because all her vitals were fine. When she was taken to her room, the nurse said that her blood pressure was high and that she was super dehydrated and immediately administered the IV. I addressed my concern about the lack of care from the emergency staff and how they lied to me that her vitals were all fine.

The following day, I had a random visit from a social worker at the hospital. I felt so offended! She came in, and before even introducing herself, she peeked in and yelled across the room to me like she was speaking to a child, "Do you speak any English?" I said, "Yes. Why?"

She came into the room and sat across the room from me. I knew that if my mother continued without having a feeding tube, she would eventually pass away. I requested a feeding tube for her. That social worker came in, and she demanded that I change my mind.

She told me that I should just let my mother "Die peacefully"!

I told her, "Absolutely not! I will fight for my mother to have the proper care!"

Then she asked me, "What country are you from? What is your mom's religion? What are her beliefs?" She did not earn her right to ask me these personal questions the way she introduced herself.

At this point, I was disappointed and did not want to answer her question.

She said, "Well, I have in the doctor's note that your mother does not want to have a feeding tube."

I said, "My mother isn't even fluent in English! I was with her on all of the visits, and she did not say that!"

She said, "But look at her, your mom, she has been bedridden, and that is not a good quality of life. You should just let her go."

The nurse who was caring for my mother turned to the social worker and said, "That's not true, I got her mom up and walking, and she just finished brushing her teeth."

While they were going back and forth, and the social worker was requesting that I end my mother's life, my mom turned to me and said in Lao, "I'm so hungry, I want to eat some chicken wings."

I said, "Does that sound like someone who wants to end their life?"

That social worker got up, throwing her hands up in the air in disappointment that I wasn't going to let my mother die. She said, "Oh! So, you've made up your mind? No matter what I say, you're going to let her live like that?"

I have a lot of patience, but she made me very upset at this point. I said to her, "Look! It is God's call when it's time for her to go, and I'm not going to allow my mother to die without a fight!"

She walked away, shaking her head, and yelled over to me while throwing her hands up, "FINE, I TRIED!"

I reached out to my friend from another Grand Rapids hospital, and she told me that I should not keep my mother there. She said I had the right to pull my mom out and take her to another hospital. I was glad to hear that, and I made them discharge her immediately and transported her to the other hospital. They took better care of her, and the next day she had a tube placed.

During this time, my husband, who is African American, worked from home, and he was helping to take care of my mother. I had a busy work schedule and attended school full time.

It was so special to see them form a special bond. They did their best to communicate. Once in a while, things would get lost in translation, but they would laugh through it! Even though my mother and husband did not fully understand each other, their bond was strong.

When my mother passed, my husband became a monk for one day to honor the Lao tradition and in honor of my mother.

We need always to remember to live and love intentionally no matter who or what life brings our way. We need to wrap our arms around our loved ones and remember to take time with our elders. We need to fight and advocate for our parents and elders, who have sacrificed so much of themselves for us. If we do not, they will be left to the fate of some strangers who may not care as much as we do.

It pains me to see all the hate against our Asian elders that is happening worldwide. I have cried many times while watching, and all I could think of was, "That could be my family."

We must remember that life is fragile, and we are not promised tomorrow. We need to live each day to the fullest and never take anything for granted.

Chapter Eight

The Misconceptions

Some people think that all Asians are born smart! the truth is, we have to work just as hard, if not harder, than most people to get ahead.

After high school, I went to beauty school against my parents' wishes. They wanted me to go to a traditional college and told me that I would not make a living as a beautician. I failed through high school and graduated with the lowest GPA that you need to graduate, and I did not feel I was college material.

Growing up, I remember my father would always say, "Honey, education is important in America. I don't want you to work hard for minimum wage like your mother and I did."

After getting my cosmetology license and instructor's license, I got my massage therapy and real estate license. It was not until I worked as a massage therapist that I learned about Asian women being fantasized!

There are so many misconceptions about Asians. Another misconception about refugees is that we were brought to America and handed a silver spoon on a platter. This is so not the case. When we come to America, if we are fortunate, we get a little help, in the beginning, to get us stable and on our feet. We are on our own after that and have to work hard just like everyone else. We must pursue our education and find a way to make a living for ourselves. Many of us are here because of the challenges we were placed in and the conditions in our homeland. We have left everything behind in search of a better life.

During the George Floyd protest of 2020, I remember having a teaching moment with someone on Facebook. I mentioned that the police officer, Derek Chauvin's ex-wife was a minority. She experienced the same journey as I did, and she was even in the refugee camps of Thailand at the same time that I was. Someone had a response that was quite eye-opening for me. She said something along the lines of, "I don't see Asians as a minority. I see you all as I see white people. Asians receive the same privilege; they don't have to pay taxes, and they receive a ton of money when they get to America." I have heard similar statements before. We had to work hard, if not harder than the average Americans. It was quite a shock that there are people out there who believe that!

As I mentioned earlier, my husband is an African American gentleman. On special occasions or sometimes "just because" he would have flowers delivered to me or he would bring them by to my job to surprise me. I have been told on several occasions by my Caucasian coworkers, "You don't look like you date black guys." I'm always shocked when I hear that, even though I hear it so often that I should be used to it. I don't know that some people are aware of the things they say and how it affects the person.

One thing to understand about the Lao community is that we are not an affectionate culture. It is rare to see a parent hug or kiss their child. While growing up, our parents rarely told us that they loved us. We were just supposed to know that they did. When we hear comments coming from our elders, it is very direct and no sugar coating. If you are fat, you are called "thuy". If you are skinny, you are called "joy". If you are white skinned, you are called "khao". If you are dark skinned, you are called "la" or "dum" and so on. Our ancestors come from small villages of Laos and most come with little or no education. Of course, things are different for those of us who have become more Americanized.

I remember when I had my oldest daughter, Asia, in 1996. She is biracial. I had people in and out of my house to come by to see my baby. They wanted to see her complexion and were surprised to see how light she was. The comments like "Oh, she took after us, she's not dark" or "Oh good, her hair is not kinky." I was very annoyed by those statements, but I knew that it was just ignorance and what they were taught.

Many people think that Asians are just born with money. I've been told, "You don't know what poor is; you were probably raised with a silver spoon!" I had to say to them, "We were so poor we ate with our fingers!"

I do hope that before passing judgment, people would take their time to educate themselves about each other's journey. We are so quick to say things that are offensive due to our lack of knowledge and understanding.

I believe that in every race, we can do a much better job at embracing our differences. We could see an end to this race war if we took the time to get to know and listen to someone different from us. When you take time to listen and connect with someone, it creates a stronger bond and unity between our two worlds, and we can finally live harmoniously as one.

I have seen the racist remarks come from all ethnicities. We all have come so far, but we have so much farther to go. I'm so grateful that things have improved over the past twenty years, but I'm hopeful for a better tomorrow.

It is also great to see the solidarity between Blacks, Asians, and others helping to rally against racism. At the same time, it still breaks my heart to see such hatred still lives among us. I know that we still have so much to learn from one another and so much further to go, but I am optimistic that we are heading in the right direction.

Chapter Nine

Breaking Through the Bamboo Ceiling

Even though I have managed to be successful in my business ventures, it was not an easy road, especially being an Asian woman in corporate. There were so many obstacles in the way. "Breaking through the Bamboo Ceiling" is a term that I heard recently on a social media app, the Clubhouse. It is a term used to describe the barriers that many Asian Americans face in the corporate arena. Despite the existence of the bamboo ceiling, there are still ways that you can break through it and find your way to success!

You must believe in yourself and know that you are capable and deserving of everything you put your mind to.

I never thought in a million years, while failing through school that I would be running one of the top-named beauty schools in the country. I managed the large campus with over two hundred students and supervised twenty staff. It only takes that one or two key people to give you a chance, and I am so grateful that they took that chance on me. The most important thing, besides that, is that I took that chance on myself. You must speak up when you see or feel you are being mistreated.

Many instances in my career have put me in an uncomfortable position. Growing up in an Asian household, you were taught to stay quiet and not cause any conflict. In some of those instances, I could not help but speak up. In one example, the results were very unfavorable and led to me getting fired for speaking up. In most instances, I was able to let my voice be heard. Sometimes you have to pick and choose your battles.

I worked for a company where I was being transitioned to another department that needed my help. Before being in that position, the former director, a Caucasian female, made fifteen to twenty thousand dollars per year more than I did. When I was being transitioned for the new job, I was helping to hire and train my replacement. We selected a Caucasian male. As I was doing his new hire paperwork, I couldn't help but notice that he was getting compensated, again, fifteen thousand dollars more annually to do my job. I know we all see things from our lens based on our experience and education. Through my lens, I couldn't help but think if I was Caucasian, would I be paid the same? I didn't speak up that time as I was just grateful for the opportunity.

I moved on to another educational institution. I was being considered for the director position to run the admissions team. This time, a bachelor's degree was required, and they said that they absolutely could not hire anyone without a bachelor's, or they would get in trouble. I had college credits that were equivalent to an associate. I was told that they couldn't offer me the director position; however, I would be considered for the admissions manager role. These were still the same duties and responsibilities as the director's role, just a different title and less compensation. I accepted the position, and when I received my offer letter, it was ten thousand less than what I was told that position paid. I brought that up to the campus president, and she said that it was because I did not have my degree.

Again, I oversaw the hiring process of the new director. We interviewed a few different candidates and ended up hiring a Caucasian female. Since I was part of her hiring process, I had access to her resume. I remember feeling upset when I saw that she also did not have a bachelor's degree. This was something they were all so adamant about, and I was offered a different position. This time, I did not stay silent. I asked about it, and I was just told that "well, she will be working toward it."

When I finally learned that I was paid much lower than one of my staff members, I spoke up again. This time, I called my VP of Admissions and let him know that I would be leaving if I did not get the pay I was supposed to get to begin with. As an Asian woman working in corporate, it is very helpful to have allies. My VP knew that I was a very hard worker, and he had my back. It also helped that he was married to an Asian woman. The campus president was very nasty toward me about it, but she gave it to me because she had to.

Well, in the words of John Maxwell, "Sometimes you win, and sometimes you learn." That was another learning moment for me. I learned to take the good with the bad and move on. I continued in that position until something better came along.

THE IGNORANCE

I left the education sector and went into the real estate industry, where I managed the leasing department for a large community. It was a demanding job, but I enjoyed the change of pace until I realized that I was once again being treated differently. A part of me wants to believe that it was unintentional. The things I experienced during my time there were eye-opening, but they didn't surprise me.

I had just started this position, and before taking over the sales team, they had an interim supervisor. The former supervisor was having an issue with an employee performing well but lacking customer service skills. We had multiple complaints from residents about this employee.

Since I am now her manager, I would have to be the one to deliver any disciplinary actions. The former supervisor wrote her up and brought the paperwork to me, stating, "Here is her write-up. I believe that you should write her up because you are a minority like she is. She won't take it as hard coming from you." She noticed the shock on my face, and she proceeded to say, "I don't mean anything by that; I'm not racist or anything. I came from a tiny town. You can bring your Asian food, she can bring her Mexican food, and I can bring my American food. I love all ethnicities." I was still a little new, so I just left it alone.

Then I started to notice different things that I did not have that other managers were privileged to. I was the only manager who worked every weekend; I was the only manager that did not have a laptop—so whenever I had to do payroll or other work-related tasks, I had to drive to the office. The big one was that I was the only manager that had to pay rent, which the other managers received free.

Other insulting things were said to me during my time working there. When I had a new community manager, I made small talk with her, and I said that she favored one of my aunts. Her response to me was, "Well, you look like this Vietnamese girl that I just fired at my last job!"

I had one incident that hit home for me. There were five of us managers in the community van. We were on our way to walk the property and inspect some of the apartments. I got in the driver's seat to drive us around the block. One of the managers sitting in the back seat yelled out loud to me, "Are you sure you can drive? I don't know how they drive in your country, but MY COUNTRY, we drive on the right-hand side—hahaha!" He burst into unstoppable laughter, and others joined him.

I didn't find it funny at all, so I was not laughing. I was dying inside, and I was trying hard to hold back the tears. It brought out emotions in me, and I visualized the bombs on our country, my uncle buried alive in front of the villagers, my father being held captive, and running for his life all started to play on my mind. I didn't let them see me crying, but I had an emotional breakdown when I was alone. Did he even know how cruel his words were? I AM an American, and I DO belong here; this IS my country!

When I spoke up about not having the same treatment as other managers, I had pushback. It wasn't until another coworker, a Caucasian, witnessed these things and reported them, that anyone did anything about it.

It may have also helped that the new VP had a husband who was a minority. She immediately transferred that manager back to where he came from, put in a request for my laptop, and offered me the free rent. I am thankful for those who look past my outer appearance and accept me for who I am.

Ironically, I had an encounter with what I felt was racism, as I was finishing my book. Perhaps it is my own imagination, but it is my reality due to my lived experiences.

I recently had a situation where I was offered a contract position to help create a sales structure for a large organization with three hundred and fifty centers. We were down to the wire, with a start date and background check all completed. They were finalizing the details of the position. A former co-worker referred me. Everyone I spoke to gave me positive feedback on how I would be an excellent asset to the team. My interactions were all by phone. Then, the last communication was with the CFO. This time it was a video conference. He appeared utterly shocked and uncomfortable to see me on video! He had little eye contact with me the entire time we were on video. I do not think that they knew "Laura Robertson" was

Asian! I hate to make it about race, but when you have experienced racism as I have, it is so hard not to.

I was told I would get a call to let me know what the new start date will be. I never received that call. Instead, I was informed by someone else that they were backtracking and considering another candidate, a Caucasian female, with less experience than I had – a person that they have already turned down once! That uncomfortable interaction with the CFO already told me that something was not right. It didn't make sense how I was given the offer, did my background check, and still – they decided to consider another candidate AFTER they saw my face. I made the decision easy. When I learned about this, I sent them an email to kindly rescind my desire to move forward with their company. This is not new to me. It is something that I have encountered time and time again. People see my name "Laura Robertson" and they do not associate that with an Asian person. Once they see my face, some people start to back paddle. I believe this was the case in this situation.

Another example was a time when I was referred to a college for a director of admissions position. I had a great phone interview with the hiring managers. I was told that they would have human resources reach out to me right away for an in-person interview. They even asked how soon I can make the drive from Elgin, IL to Michigan for my interview.

Shortly after the phone call, the hiring manager looked me up on LinkedIn. LinkedIn has a feature that shows you who looks up your profile picture. The very next morning, I received one of those default letters, "we have found someone else that fits that position and will keep your resume on file...etc." I could not help but think that it was because I was Asian.

I cannot prove that the people involved had ill intentions behind their actions, but with my negative past experiences, it leads me to think that way.

I know that racism does exist. I wish I could take a blind eye to it, but I cannot because I have experienced it on many occasions. Because of my experience with racism throughout my life, I notice things that others may not be aware of.

My advice to those who have never experienced racism, is to please be mindful of how your actions, whether intentional or not, could come across to someone that may be looking at things from a different lens. Some of us have things that happened to us in the past that we may not have healed from. Please be open and understanding.

Despite all the roadblocks, it does not stop me from pushing myself. I continue to focus only on the things that matter, connect with the people who believe in me, serve the ones that God placed on my path to serve, and pray each day for a more loving world.

As a praying woman of faith, I know that every rejection is only a redirection to something greater. It is all a part of God's way of preventing me from going down the wrong path. Those who treated me unfairly because of my ethnic background, do not define me. The amazing people who believed in me, who gave me a chance and helped me "break through the bamboo ceiling", those are the ones that I will always remember!

Chapter Ten

My Mother's Goodbye

I always promised my mother that I would never put her in a nursing home and that I would be the one to take care of her. I kept my promise, and we kept her home, taking turns to care for her for four years until she took her last breath. I will never forget her last words to me. My mother was not a very empathetic person. She seldom expressed her emotions, and I believe it's due to the hard life she led.

It was on a Sunday when I was leaving to catch a flight for work. I went to see her, and she was struggling with the shingles on top of all her other medical issues. She looked fragile, and it seemed she knew that she didn't have much fight left in her. After I fed her, I tucked her in bed, and I kissed her on her cheeks. I could see her eyes filled up with tears. She looked up at me and said, "I lub you" (I love you). I told her that I loved her but immediately knew something was wrong. I felt that she was giving up, and this was her way of telling me. That Wednesday, I received a call from my father that mom had passed away in her sleep.

I remember at her funeral, one of my aunts said something to me that stood out. I didn't know if anyone else knew about the conflict I had with my mother as a teenager, that I did not turn out to be the daughter that she had imagined. My aunt turned to me and said, "Here we are. It's so crazy how life works. I know that when you were younger, you were the daughter that your mother was disappointed with, and she put your brothers on a pedestal. Look how things turned out in the end. You are the one who was there for her, waiting on your mother hand and foot for years, sacrificing so much for her until her last breath. I know that your mother left here with a smile on her face and feeling proud of the woman you became."

I was told by so many people that my future was a lost cause and I would never amount to anything. I'm glad that I did not let those words define me, and I followed my dreams. I vow to continue to do what makes me happy. If I am breathing, I will continue to give back and help others reach for their dreams. I will continue to keep my mother's dream alive; I will continue to embrace our culture; I will make sure that all the sacrifices she made for us to have a better life were not in vain.

I am so glad that my mother could be here to see the highlights of my career and that she saw with her own two eyes that all three of her children were successful in the end.

My brother Nor is a successful marketing manager and illustrator. He has published a children's book and illustrated another. His painting of Obama's visit to Laos will be in the Obama museum. My other brother, Alisak, works in IT at the University of Merced. He also produces his wife's YouTube channel "Cooking with Nana." My mother left this world knowing that all her blood, sweat, and tears for her children to have a better future came to fruition, and all her sacrifices were not in vain.

Chapter Eleven

This Is My Country

With what my family sacrificed to come to America, it deeply saddens me that as Asian Americans, we still have to fight for our place in America.

The more education and awareness we bring, the more it will help get us closer and closer to ending racism.

Since the pandemic, there has been a rise in violence against Asians. I did not know that we would be facing all this during the pandemic; that racism and prejudice we encounter now would be unfolding. This book was just perfect timing for what our Asian communities are facing right now with the #stopasianhate protest.

My father, a soldier that had to kill or be killed, is scared to go outside of his home. He thought that bringing us here, we were safe from the enemies, but here in America, we fight a new enemy—RACISM.

I remember the joy on my father's face one day when I came to visit him. He pulled me over to the wall, pointed to a plaque he had received, and with a big smile on his face he said, "Look at this!"

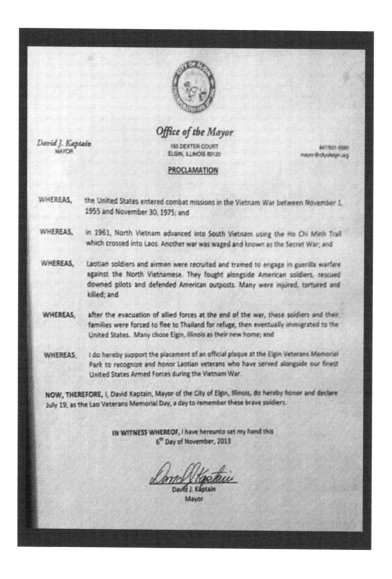

I got super emotional as I read the plaque. It was almost surreal! This was a plaque to honor my father and other Laotian soldiers that fought alongside and protected the American soldiers during the Vietnam War.

The plaque signed by Mayor David Kaptain, on November 6th, 2013, wrote:

WHEREAS, the United States entered combat missions in the Vietnam War between November 1, 1955 and November 30, 1975; and

WHEREAS, in 1961, North Vietnam advanced into South Vietnam using the Ho Chi Minh Trail which crossed into Laos, another war was waged and known as the Secret War; and

WHEREAS, Laotian soldiers and airmen were recruited and trained to engage in guerilla warfare against the North Vietnamese. They fought alongside American soldiers, recued downed pilots and defended American outposts. Many were injured, tortured and killed; and

WHEREAS, after the evacuation of allied forces at the end of the war, these soldiers and their families were forced to flee to Thailand for refuge, then eventually immigrated to the United States. Many chose Elgin, Illinois as their new home; and

WHEREAS, I do hereby support the placement of an official plaque at the Elgin Veterans Memorial Park to recognize and honor Laotian veterans who have served alongside our finest United States Armed Forces during the Vietnam War.

NOW, THEREFORE, I, David Kaptain, Mayor of the City of Elgin, Illinois, do hereby honor and declare July 19, as the Lao Veterans Memorial Day, a day to remember these brave soldiers.

On my birthday, May 3rd, 2021, I attended a ribbon cutting to kick off Asian American & Pacific Islander Heritage Month at the Elgin Gail Borden Library. That day I had an opportunity to meet Mayor David Kaptain and State Representative, Anna Moeller. Mrs. Moeller announced another huge milestone. She shared with us that Illinois recently passed legislation that the teaching of Asian American history will be required for all schools. I am so grateful for this and for the city of Elgin. They have done a wonderful job welcoming and helping our Lao community. I hope that this will bring more education and end the hate against our Asian communities.

I had one encounter during the pandemic where I was standing in line. Even though I was six feet away from a Caucasian gentleman, he still flung his cane at me, and with anger in his face, he yelled for me to "get back further!" We were both wearing masks. Then I stepped away and let the next person behind me go before me. The following person in line stepped on the six-foot mark where I was standing when I got chased away but did not get the same treatment. They were also Caucasian. It's hard when a country, the only country that I know and give my all to, has people who tell us to go back to "our country."

I have heard people say, "racism is made up" or "racism doesn't exist." Until you experience it for yourself, you will not know that it does exist. I have had my fair share of mistreatment being Asian in American. Out of all this hate, I still see love flourish. There are so many people who are loving. I refuse to let the hatred of a few dictate the love of the many supporting us being here.

Racism exists in all communities. I have seen and experienced it with my own eyes for myself from every race. Sometimes it is intentional hate, and other times it is the ignorance of people who are uneducated or unaware of how their words affect others.

My husband has also encountered racism toward me from his black acquaintances. They question "How can you be pro-Black if you are with an Asian wife?"

The recent Atlanta spa shooting that left eight people dead including six Asian women, has me believing that we need more media representation in the Asian community. The suspect claimed that he was "sexually frustrated and having a bad day." This led him on a shooting spree at Asian spas taking innocent lives. We need to change the narrative that Asian women are only good for sexual pleasures. We are so much more than that!

My kids, being mixed race, get it from all sides as well. We all have work to do, and we need more dialogue and discussions to support and understanding each other. We need to learn more about people who are different from us. Due to the pandemic and both of our communities (Black and Asian) being the most vilified races, my husband and I started a podcast, "Blasian Soul Podcast" www.blasiansoulpodcast.com. Our goal is to do our part to shine the light on current events and bring out the good things that are happening and change the narrative in the Black and Asian communities.

Today, as I write this book, on April 22, the COVID-19 hate crimes Act against Asian Americans passed in the US. Maybe, just maybe, this will be the beginning of less fear and more justice for our community.

Chapter Twelve

My Career Highlights

I finally left my corporate position on December 10, 2019, to pursue my dreams. I loved the work that I was doing, and I was compensated very well for it. However, there was this strong desire to pursue my dreams of helping others climb the success. I had just hit the highest pay grade in my entire life, with $213,205.62 gross for the year! But I decided to leave because I felt this strong calling to do something more.

I never thought in a million years that I would achieve the level of success that I was able to reach. I was always told that I would never amount to anything and that my future was a lost cause. When I was a troubled teen or a single mother on welfare, it never crossed my mind that I would come this far. Many times, I would sit there in amazement! Finally, I decided that I did not want to keep this feeling to myself. I wanted to help others climb their ladder of success and reach their potential. That was when my consulting company, Beautiful Potential Consulting, was born.

I wanted to show that you do not have to come from a wealthy household or be of a particular race and ethnic group to reach your potential. You do not have to be the most intelligent person to earn a good living or follow your dreams. If you are open to learning, if you are coachable, if you aim to serve others, and if you want it bad enough – it is your God-given right to have it!

I want to be an example that we are not limited by who we are or how others define us. I want you to know that you have the unlimited power to live the life of your dreams no matter your past or current circumstances.

I want anyone living in poverty, especially those who shared a similar struggle as a Southeast Asian American, to see that no matter where you came from, how much money, or lack of, that we were born into—we all have the power in our hands to change our circumstances and live out our dreams!

I have worked in sales, coaching, leadership, and management, and a variety of fields. I found my passion to be in coaching and development. I love giving the tools to help others become the best version of themselves. I became an independent certified coach, speaker, and trainer with The John Maxwell Group.

I created my business, Beautiful Potential Consulting, to provide a platform that I can use to empower clients to grow personally and professionally. Beautiful Potential Consulting is a beauty, branding, and business consulting company. Beautiful Potential also provides an online school where anyone can take classes at their own pace. The courses range from business to branding courses such as social media marketing, video marketing, business training, and a step-by-step tutorial to help grow your business. I believe that the more you know, the more you grow!

I also co-own a marketing and advertising company, iLocal Online Marketing, with my husband.

Since my business started when the pandemic hit, I have been using this time to build my business platform and speak on virtual platforms to share my story. My story has been shared on several different media outlets, podcasts and featured on the cover of the March edition of a women's magazine called *Her Story Matters*.

One project I was blessed to be a part of was the making of the *Lao Redemption*. This was a film by Mychal Mitchel of Northshore Films. It is a fictional story depicting what happened during the secret war on Laos. The movie is about seven CIA agents who went undercover to find out who initiated the bombings on our country.

Bronx Obama, an Obama impersonator, played the role of the real Obama. In real life, former President Obama was the first sitting President to visit Laos and acknowledge the US involvement in the bombings on our country. The reminiscence of the bombs is still killing our farmers and children in Laos. He also assigned relief funds to help aid the clean-up of the unexploded bombs. It will take more than a lifetime to get rid of these bombs, but I am glad that we are moving in the right direction.

Working on the movie took me back down memory lane. We filmed a flashback scene in the Elgin area where I grew up, a barefoot, poor refugee child in America. Some of my refugee pictures were also used throughout the movie. It is now playing on Vimeo on Demand.

The American dream is here for everyone. So let us work together to share, educate, and spread love to those who are different from us. Let us work together to make this a more peaceful, harmonious world to live in. Let us be open to be better listeners and understand those views that are different than ours. Let us look to ourselves and make sure our hearts are in the right place; let us find opportunities and teaching moments so that we can all move towards a better place than where we are now.

WE all have the power and responsibility in our hands to make a change.

Together, we can ALL live the *American Dream!*

Get in Touch!
Instagram & FB: @businesscoachlaura

www.beautifulpotential.com
www.ilocalonlinemarketing.com
www.businesscoachlaura.com
www.blasiansoulpodcast.com

Made in the USA
Columbia, SC
02 December 2021